Between *Ardh* and *Samawaat*

Physicals, non-physicals

and in-between

A Qur'anic Perspective

ZUBAIR KAREEM

To contact the author, email:
BCAL2013@yahoo.com

Paperback ISBN#: 978-0-9891073-6-5
Ebook ISBN#: 978-0-9891073-7-2

Cover and interior design:
Deborah Perdue
https:illuminationgraphics.com

Dedication

Dedicated to all *seekers,*
Especially those who ask questions

Zubair Kareem

A thinker, writer, and seeker—of truth.

Previous works:

Between Cruelty and Love

Muslims' Intellectual Eclipse

Islamic Finance and the Riba

Contents

Chapter 1

Introduction

IN THE NAME OF ALLAH, the Most Gracious the Most Merciful.

I remember and recognize Him, *subhanahu wa ta'ala (SWT)* – the Most Glorified, the Most Exalted, being the Most Knowledgeable and the Originator of everything. His creations include everything we can ever think about or discover, closest to our own selves or in the farthest expanse of His creations. Out of His Mercy, He bestowed messengers, the prophets, upon us for guidance, especially His last Prophet Muhammad, *sallallahu alaihi wasallam* (SAW)– peace and blessings of Allah (SWT) be upon him.

Allah (SWT) is the Creator and the Sustainer of our individual and collective minds, our consciousness and our thoughts. With limited freedom within our reach, our abilities are constantly tested. In intellectual terms, trying to find answers for practical and philosophical questions is in our instinct or in our "DNA". Based upon circumstances and abilities, some of us do it more and some less. The very first revealed message of the Quran was, *Iqra*, usually translated as, *Read*. Its implied message is larger: Gather information by observation, reading or any other means; reflect and critique, like the Prophet Ibrahim, *alaihi salam (AS)* – peace be upon him, did. If done right, to our benefit, it may open new ideological and practical avenues for us, if Allah (SWT) wills. We are asked to put our best efforts. At the end, all this effort is to get closer to Him, to know Him better by reflecting on His abilities and creations.

Based upon our ability or tendency to *read*, as defined above, an individual can broadly be described as either a *conformist* or a *nonconformist*. Most people in the world, as well as most societies and nations, fall into the first category of being conformists. They are either indifferent, or satisfied with their situations, are following the prevailing ideologies, and continuing with actions and routines of their ancestors or peers. Sometimes, motives are more selfish and material based. In nature—or if people were left entirely to themselves—a small percentage of any society belongs to the latter group, the nonconformists. This group perceives things differently. They are not content with the prevailing ideologies and may not be satisfied with what they witness or experience. Not only that they may disapprove a prevailing idea or a practice, but they also come up with alternate and newer concepts. Depending upon the field or the place they might be working at, they are the pioneers or reformers, sometimes revolutionaries. On practical level, with their maverick approach, they innovate and invent. With rightly guided vision and conducive environment, they may become the backbone of progress and success of their respective societies. If ignored or abused, their God-given talent may be lost, which is a major issue in so-many struggling societies all around the globe. Promoting and grooming these individuals and their approach is exponentially beneficial, both to them and their societies This group of people brings upon change and has the capacity to lead and reach a higher level in all areas of human understanding and endeavor: Ideological, practical, or spiritual. Recognizing their value, some societies have intentionally charted a different course and tried to increase their number and influence. The United States is one such example.

What many people don't realize is that after the so-called II World War, the U.S. government deliberately set out to guide future generations toward creativity and innovation. That is why, across disciplines—from the arts and language to science—schools, colleges, and universities implemented curricula and culture designed to encourage creativity. Fundamental requirement for creativity and innovation is independent and critical thinking, which was promoted and rewarded. This, in large part, explains why American society has been more successful than many others. Other nations that have adopted a similar approach have achieved comparable success.

In the U.S., the proportion of people who might be considered inventors—in any aspect of human endeavor or expression—used to be small but has been steadily increasing. It is probably close to 40/60 or 50/50 now: Little more than half of Americans can still be described as primarily conformist, while the others are nonconformist; be it small, in their thinking, actions, and life paths. Children growing up and educated in this environment think and behave differently, especially from those where most of the immigrants come from. For example, most immigrant parents do not understand value of the so-called, Liberal Arts college education and prefer more technical and STEM fields for their children. Even in applied fields, they struggle to understand proper application and use of this type of education beyond the scope of an employment.

This situation creates a mental conflict of a sort between parents and their children, a conflict that can manifest in all areas of their lives: academic, social, and religious.

For Muslims, there is another layer of problem. In most settings, Islamic institutions or the local masjid does not promote independent and critical thinking. On the contrary, frequently and in both explicit and implicit terms, they promote conformism. Speakers are frequently hostile to the idea of not conforming with what is stated or conventionally understood, even if it makes no logical sense. Children and reflective adults, especially teen-agers, feel disconnected and alienated in these institutions. They may come to pray and attend other events but stay mostly reclusive and often frustrated. Even for routine and well-established practices and ideas, many, who wanted to learn, click to the online platform. Even on that forum, conformism is the prevailing standard but there is some alternate material, here and there, but not to the extent to have a meaningful impact. Reasons for this situation are many, including the lack of proper training and ingrained ideologies of the religious leadership, most of whom are trained in institutions with a very different culture.

Here and there, people put a private or a separate effort to meet, read and reflect. Though libraries are available, most seldom go to such places. These events become a mixture of social and educational gatherings, with food being the key component. In individual settings, people are more attached to the phone in their hand than any other object or location. Even that activity is mostly for fun, or what some call, 'cyber *sawab*'. People are circulating Islamic messages, including *Hadith* and *ayat* of the Qur'an, maybe to have a sense of performing a good deed. Some go little deeper or spend more time and listen to online lectures and opinions. This practice is not only about religious matters, but other matters are also dealt in the same manner. Culture of book reading, researching, critiquing and reflecting, which was the intended message of the word *Iqra*, is sparse, selective or private.

For the subject of religion, this may take the form of a Quran *Halaqa*. But that effort, depending how it is conducted, may also mirror the same approach as outlined above, albeit in a different forum. In our small town of South Hadley, we have tried to take a different approach. In this setting, exploration and critical thinking is promoted. An effort is made to avoid conformism, without knowing and understanding the alternate scholarly point of view. This is done with a hope that we all apply this approach to our daily lives while addressing different religious and non-religious matters. Material of this book has come out of those settings and the questions raised. It may help to understand and reflect on certain topics applicable to our day-to-day life but especially to understanding the Qur'an. The largest section is devoted to the chapter on *ardh* and *samawaat,* a ubiquitous subject in the Qur'an. May Allah (SWT) keep us away from falsehood and open the door for truth. May He accept this small effort.

Chapter 2

Truth and Truthfulness

TRUTHFULNESS IS THE FUNDAMENTAL and arguably the most critical Islamic trait. The Prophet Muhammad (SAW) spent 40 years among his community exhibiting exemplary character, earning the titles *"the truthful and the trustworthy"* (*As-Sadiq, Al-Amin*), even before receiving revelation. Any belief or explanation loses its merit if it is rooted in falsehood. Truth particularly matters when its declaration could compromise one's own position. The Qur'an is unequivocally clear on this:

Al-Qur'an 4:135 *"O you who believe! Stand out firmly for justice, as witnesses to Allah, even if it be against yourselves, your parents, or your kin, and whether it be against rich or poor: for Allah can best* *protect both. Do not follow your own desires, lest you swerve, and if you distort or decline to do justice—verily, Allah is well-acquainted with all that you do."*

Al-Qur'an 9:119 *"O you who believe! Fear Allah and be with those who are true (in word and deed)."*

A person who does not speak the truth or recognize its virtue may not have taken the first step toward being a Muslim. Being Muslim requires understanding Allah (SWT) and His supreme position. HE knows what is within us—our thoughts, intentions, and values. With that understanding, lying, fabricating, or cheating is incompatible with Islam.

Al-Qur'an 10:61 *"There is no activity you may be engaged in [O Prophet], or portion of the Quran you may be reciting, nor any deed you all may be doing, except that We are a Witness over you while doing it. Not even an atom's weight is hidden from your Lord on earth or in heaven—nor anything smaller or larger—but it is [written] in a perfect Record."*

Some might argue that certain situations call for a more flexible approach. For example, if a host serves a meal that is less than delicious and then asks for our opinion, it is better to find something kind to say rather than bluntly stating the truth. In our daily interactions with spouses, families, and friends, such tact is often appreciated. However, this leniency does not extend to lying to one's spouse about where one spent the evening or the unexplained loss of thousands from a joint account. Such behavior breaches the core of trust.

Another area of confusion concerns the very nature of truth. What exactly *is* truth for a human being, and how do we determine it? Some attempt to separate truth into "religious" and "non-religious" domains, suggesting different standards may apply. While in many everyday matters, it is relatively easy to identify truth, the waters become murkier when we address deeper, existential or metaphysical questions.

Let us first consider the religious dimension. We Muslims believe in Allah (SWT), His messengers, His books, the angels, the hereafter, and accountability. For us, these are absolute truths. On the other hand, non-Muslims or a non-believers may not agree. One of the disagreements and the concept difficult to fully grasp is the notion of resurrection after death, which, using "logic" or conventional physics is difficult to prove. This subject is addressed multiple times in the Quran:

Al-Qur'an 36:78–79 *"And they argue with Us—forgetting their own creation—saying, 'Who will give life to decayed bones?' Say, [O Prophet], 'They will be revived by the One Who created them the first time. He has perfect knowledge of every created being.'"*

In matters of belief, we accept these truths by faith. We support our position by reflective logic, and sometimes our "unexplainable" experiences in life. Belief in the afterlife and the accountability is not easy—but it is critical to understand the overall human situation. All of this remains a matter of belief with reflective circumstantial evidence, instead of a physical prove. The Qur'an also notes that even the disbelievers will one day acknowledge the truth, while witnessing the prove:

Al-Qur'an 32:12 *"If only you could see the wicked hanging their heads in shame before their Lord, [crying:] 'Our Lord! We have now seen and heard. So send us back and we will do good. We truly have sure faith now!'"*

Now, consider non-religious matters, particularly science. Science is a continuing quest for truth. Scientists may dismiss religious claims as unproven, while religious individuals may criticize science for its evolving conclusions. Both seek truth—but often talk past one another due to a fundamental misunderstanding: For humans, truth is frequently tentative and evolving. To be certain about something, especially about fundamental principles, is not entirely a fixed concept.

Islamic thought recognizes three levels of certainty, as described in the Quran:

a. *'Ilm al-Yaqīn* (Certainty through information gathering):

This is the level of certainty that comes from circumstantial evidence or indirect information. For instance, if someone says that there is an animal in a room, based upon signs of its existence he may have found without seeing the animal, we may not doubt it. In some cases, if it was possible and depending upon the animal, we may even go inside the room and confirm those signs ourselves. In that case, we might not have seen the animal either, but we might get better convinced of the animal's existence. The level of certainty in many domains of human knowledge, from biology to atomic physics, our understanding rarely exceeds this level.

b. *'Ayn al-Yaqīn* (Certainty through seeing or experiencing):

This is certainty gained through direct observation or experience—like seeing the above-described animal in the room. However, for a lot many things, this level of certainty is often elusive. We have never truly "seen" an atom, especially its sub-particles; we accept their existence through indirect evidence. When we see stars at night, we are only witnessing their ancient light reaching to us billions of years after it was emitted. Whether those stars still exist is unknown—we would have to travel to them to reach this level of certainty, which seems impossible for our existence, or at least our present scientific understandings. Similarly, with multiple limitations of our vision, we have a problem when trying to directly see an atom or a subatomic particle. But most of us, do not deny their existence, due to the indirect proof or evidence we may gather or accept.

For some of us, truth may sometimes differ from our previous understandings or pre-conceived notions. Instead of changing our positions, many of us use a futile argument to counter this level of certainty. For example, people who do not accept that humans have landed on the moon, or the earth is not flat, are making this type of mistake.

c. ***Ḥaqq al-Yaqīn*** **(Absolute Truth):**

This is the ultimate, undoubted reality. For many matters, especially metaphysical ones, this level of certainty in this life remains beyond human reach or comprehension. On one hand, a doubter of the planet Earth's round shape may change his mind if taken to the space and shown the planet earth from a different perspective. On the other, we have no means to travel billions of lightyears away to reach this level of certainty about existence of a distant star.

From science, sociology & religion, we debate about the nature of things, or their true nature. No one group can claim authority on this subject and no group, including scientific and religious groups, escapes this problem. Perhaps the most debated topic in human history is the existence of God—Allah (SWT). By Islamic definition, Allah is beyond our full comprehension. We try to know Him through His signs, by exploring ourselves and the universe around us, and by reflecting on the *ardh* and the *samawaat* (to be discussed in a later chapter). In this manner, we may be convinced of His existence and may reach the limits of *ilm al-Yaqin.*

Al-Qur'an 41:53 *"We will show them Our signs in the universe and within themselves until it becomes clear to them that this 'Quran' is the truth. Is it not enough that your Lord is a Witness over all things?"*

Allah (SWT) acknowledges our limitations. When Prophet Moses (AS) requests to have a direct encounter with Allah, he is informed of the impossibility due to limitation of his existence:

Al-Quran 7:143 *When Moses came at the appointed time and his Lord spoke to him, he asked, "My Lord! Reveal Yourself to me so I may see You." Allah answered, "You cannot see Me! But look at the mountain. If it remains firm in its place, only then will you see Me." When his Lord appeared to the mountain, He levelled it to dust and Moses collapsed unconscious. When he recovered, he cried, "Glory be to You! I turn to You in repentance and I am the first of the believers."*

On the other hand, after this encounter, Prophet Moses solidified belief in Allah (SWT).

In other *ayat*, the Qur'an assures that we will all eventually meet our Lord and reach higher level of certainty about Him:

Al-Quran 75:22–23 *"Some faces that Day will be radiant, looking at their Lord."*

Al-Quran 84:6 *"O human! You are certainly laboring towards your Lord—with great exertion—then you will meet Him."*

Reflecting on this subject, one may realize that we all are at different levels of appreciation of Allah SWT's existence. Even Prophet Moses AS, in his worldly life, could only reach a certain level of certainty. This appreciation has the effect like that of best of musk, some have more, which may be easily noticeable, while some less and have subtle, and some might even less. In both belief and social matters, many people adopt a passive stance. They may know or privately accept the truth but remain silent or indifferent. Yet Allah (SWT) clearly defines the path of righteousness:

Al-Qur'an 39:33–35 *"And the one who has brought the truth and those who embrace it—it is they who are the righteous. They will have whatever they desire with their Lord. That is the reward of the good-doers. Thus, Allah will absolve them of even the worst of what they did and reward them according to the best of what they used to do."*

Finally, in the conventional scientific terms, scientists reflect on the fundamental or the basic nature of everything, from largest to the smallest particle or anything even basic, like a wave. This is where the science or the physics seems to break apart from its more logical or the Newtonian understandings to an area that transcends the concepts of space and time. This is where the concept of physical matter and non-physical entities merge, leading to a unified concept. The reader is encouraged to read about basics of quantum physics or listen to some related lectures easily available online.

Scientists speculate or theorize about the origin of our universe, the only universe known to us. Does it have a timeline? What was there before it? How did it come into being? How is it sustained? What or who is sustaining it? Philosophers, scientific and non-scientific alike, have also contemplated upon the ultimate nature or reality of everything that exists, or what we may call the ultimate truth. Numerous ancient and modern philosophers, including many Muslim scholars, have tried to come up with an explanation. More noticeable in the latter grout are Al-Farabi, Ibn-Sina, Al-Ghazali, and Ibn-Arabi, all opining on this subject. Mentioning their views, even an outline of their views, is beyond the scope of this writing. It can easily be explored online. In an indirect manner, the

Quran also provides an outline on this subject, including the following ayah:

Al-Quran 31:30 *"That is because Allah is the [only] Reality, and what they call upon besides Him is falsehood; and He is the Most High, the Most Great."*

The issue of origin and creation is discussed in the Quran in many ways. Some references are as follows: The Originator (6:101, 39:62, 59:24), creation by His command (36:82), origin of *ardh* and *samawaat* (21:30, 41:11), origin of life (24:45), origin of human being (25:54, 15:26, 32:7-9), continuity of creation (55:29, 29:19-20), and the end of everything (2:156, 11:123). All these topics are worthy of reading, researching and reflection. Taking the topic of *ardh* and *samawaat* as mentioned in the Qur'an, I have tried to address a small part of this subject in a following chapter. May Allah SWT provide guidance.

Chapter 3

How to Interpret the Quran

METAPHORICALLY SPEAKING, I'VE ALWAYS believed it's better to learn how to fish than to hope someone brings me one—or, to put it differently, it's better to learn or teach how to find the right path than to force someone onto the path I happen to be on. The core issue here is: *How should one interpret the Qur'an, or a particular ayah (verse) of it?*

I am by no means a scholar of the Qur'an. Much has been written on this topic—indeed, volumes. For English-speaking or American readers, this topic is particularly well explored in the latter part of the book, *The Study Quran*, an important contemporary resource.

Reading and understanding the Qur'an is, in part, a personal effort and, in a greater part, a special mercy or blessing from Allah (SWT). Yet the latter remains elusive without proper attention to the former. The Quran is in Arabic—more precisely, a classical form of Arabic no longer spoken in daily life. While understanding Arabic is undoubtedly helpful, numerous translations by English-speaking scholars from both the East and West—spanning generations and ethnicities—have given us a rich body of interpretive literature. This allows even non-Arabic speakers to engage deeply with the Quran. Everyone on this journey is at a certain level of understanding. No one, except the Prophet Muhammad (SAW), can claim to fully grasp its entirety. What I know is that the door of understanding begins to open only with sincere intention and consistent, formal effort.

In my view, the *ayat* (verses) of the Quran can be categorized by their subject matter as follows:

1. **Foundational** – Addressing core beliefs of Islam: the attributes of Allah (SWT), His Oneness (*Tawheed*), the Unseen (*Ghaib*), the Afterlife, the Garden or the Paradise (*Jannah*), and the Hell (*Jahannam*).

2. **Historical** – Though not a history book, the Quran recounts many historical events, often to provide moral, ideological, or comparative lessons.

3. **Parables** – Symbolic narratives conveying deeper spiritual meanings.

4. **Reminders/Instructional** – Repeated exhortations about different aspects of *Tawheed,* righteous actions, prayer, charity, etc.

5. **Rules and Regulations** – Explicit directions or broad principles on what is permissible and forbidden, though not exhaustive in scope.

6. **Scientific** – Verses that touch upon natural phenomena, encouraging rational inquiry and contemplation.

7. **Miraculous** – While the Quran in its entirety is a miracle, some verses are particularly striking in their miraculous nature, especially at the time of their revelation.

8. **Supplications** – Duas are found throughout the Quran, from the earliest chapters to the last.

9. **Miscellaneous** – E.g., mysterious lettered verses like "*Alif, Laam, Meem.*"

To interpret any *ayah*, I follow a method akin to peeling away layers of meaning:

First Layer – The immediate context of revelation.
Example: When the ayah on *khamr* (intoxicants) was revealed, Muslims stopped consuming the alcoholic beverages available at that time.

Second Layer – The same context, later times.
Example: A few years later, the message was further clarified and all forms of intoxicants including alcoholic beverages were clearly prohibited.

Third Layer – Similar, though not identical context in later times.
Example: The same *ayah* is now used to justify the prohibition of substances like opium, heroin, and cocaine.

Fourth Layer – Analogous but different contexts in later times.
Example: The *ayah* might be used to discourage or outlaw making of digital content that may intoxicate the mind or alter consciousness.

Fifth Layer – Linguistic depth and nuance.
While language is essential at all layers, here we explore grammatical, etymological, and rhetorical dimensions—for example, in interpreting *Surah Al-Balad* and its references to slavery.

Sixth Layer – Scientific or mathematical analysis. Rare and less discussed, this layer might include numerological insights or thematic structures—like those explored in *Surah Al-Qadr* during Ramadan. This type of analysis might discover hitherto unknown knowledge.

Seventh Layer – Spiritual significance, probably the most significant.
Example: The concept of *qalb* (heart) and its metaphorical role in human transformation.

Two further layers are beyond our reach:

Eighth Layer – The level of understanding granted to the Prophet Muhammad (SAW).

Ninth, the Ultimate Layer – The complete, divine understanding that rests solely with Allah (SWT).

Two Critical Misunderstandings About the Quran

It is human nature to avoid topics that provoke uncertainty or discomfort. This applies equally in religious and secular circles. People often resist ideas that challenge long-standing understandings or assumptions. As the saying goes, "Old scientists don't change their views; they just die." In religious circles, this resistance becomes more acute when a generational interpretation of a sacred text is called into question. But when outdated interpretations no longer make sense, they must be re-examined—or they risk undermining the very foundation of belief.

Here, I address two problematic assumptions:

A. That some *ayat* of the Quran have been revoked or are no longer valid.
B. That the early generations of Muslims had unquestionable understanding of the Quran.

Both views, in my opinion, are indefensible.

On Abrogation

It's true that the Quran mentions abrogation:

Al-Baqarah 2:106 – *"None of Our revelations do We abrogate or cause to be forgotten, but We substitute something better or similar. Do you not know that Allah has power over all things?"*

However, no verse in the Quran explicitly states that any *abrogated* verse remains within its final text. Nor do I find any such claim in the Hadith literature.

By contrast, several verses underscore the Quran's completeness and preservation:

Al-Hijr 15:9 – *"We have, without doubt, sent down the Message, and We will assuredly guard it from corruption."*
Al-Kahf 18:1 – *"Praise be to Allah, Who has sent to His servant the Book and has allowed therein no crookedness."*

An-Nisa 4:82 – *"Do they not ponder the Quran carefully? Had it been from other than Allah, they would surely have found in it many contradictions."*

To claim that some parts of the Quran are invalid creates a theological and logical problem. Who decides which verses are no longer valid? Early scholars proposed differing lists of "abrogated" verses, but no consensus ever formed. In fact, such interpretations led to division and sectarianism.

While certain *ayat* indicate a change in practice or policy (e.g., the change of the *Qibla* direction), they do not imply the verse itself is invalid or should be disregarded. Rather, the Quran uses such events to guide evolving understanding—not to erase prior guidance.

On the Authority of Early Generations

Prophet Muhammad (SAW) was the first person to provide explanation of the *ayat* of the Quran. After his passing, some of his close associates, who were already known for their distinct ability, continued this work, but mostly in oral tradition. First full written or documented exegesis or explanation of the Quran happened about 100 years of Prophet's passing. Since then, at different time of history and geographical locations, hundreds of scholars, if not thousands, have taken this task and provided their point of view.

This fact by itself affirms that exegesis or explanation of the Quran is a dynamic process.

The notion that a scholar's interpretation is beyond scrutiny is neither supported by the Quran nor consistent with intellectual honesty. A careful reading of various scholars reveals this clearly. Reading some translations that were done centuries ago, it is not uncommon to encounter explanation of an *ayah,* which is difficult to defend considering our current understanding of nature. In addition to that, throughout the Quran, certain themes and subjects recur frequently, appearing on almost every page. Despite their prevalence, our understanding of some of these topics remains incomplete. The reader may appreciate this issue in the chapter on *ardh* and *samawaat.* Repetition of these concepts highlights their importance and the depth of meaning they carry, inviting ongoing reflection and study. However, the full scope and significance of these themes are not always immediately clear, underscoring the dynamic and evolving nature of Quranic interpretation. Even when addressing verses that concern realities beyond human experience, scholars often include their own interpretations after citing those of earlier commentators. Therefore, each generation must engage with the Quran anew—with sincerity of intention, humility of effort, and a rational examination of the insights of those who came before. The process of reflection and interpretation is dynamic, not static. May Allah SWT bless scholarly efforts, and anyone on the path of learning and reflecting, with hope of passing on the knowledge to the next generations. Amen.

Chapter 4

The Qalb 101

IN ISLAMIC TERMINOLOGY, THE *QALB* is a spiritual concept, distinct from the physical heart. To grasp its nature, it's helpful to understand two related spiritual faculties: **intellect** and **intelligence**.

Intellect: The Seed of Understanding

Intellect is the inborn, God-given capacity to acquire knowledge. Rooted in our genetic makeup, it functions through the brain—our mental hardware and software. Just as the eyes are for seeing and the skin for touch, there is a part of the brain designated for intellect.

Although human brains may appear similar, each one is unique. This uniqueness gives every person a distinct type and level of intellect. Much like our faces or fingerprints, our intellects resemble one another yet remain fundamentally different. Notably, these differences are not determined by gender, ethnicity, skin color, geography, or wealth.

Intellect is not exclusive to humans. Animals, too, possess it—albeit to a lesser extent. Creatures like chimpanzees, keas, crows, and octopuses demonstrate remarkable intellectual capacities, though none surpass those of a human child. Even bees, in some ways, outperform many of these animals. There is even emerging evidence suggesting that plants and trees exhibit a form of intellect. However, comparing these life forms using human standards is inherently limited and potentially biased.

Due to differences in intellectual type, people excel in various fields—some in the arts, others in science or agriculture. A person gifted in drawing may be a more effective architect than an engineer. Levels of intellect vary, but they can be misunderstood or underappreciated if the type is not recognized. On the other hand, like a powerful engine alone doesn't make a car move—it needs many other parts, intellect alone does not ensure success.

Intelligence: The Use of Intellect

Intelligence is the ability to understand and apply knowledge—it reflects how intellect is utilized. For instance, someone may know the names of every part of a car but have no idea how they function together. That may be a sign of good intellect, but it is not intelligence.

True intelligence involves not just acquiring knowledge but understanding and applying it appropriately. In our context, a person may be described as an *alim* (informed), *arif* (knowledgeable), or *hakeem* (wise), depending on their level of intelligence.

While intellect is inherent and foundational, intelligence can be nurtured and developed through reflection, experience, exploration, reading & education, travel, good company, and proper guidance. The opposite is also true: Someone born with good intellect may not reach their full potential if raised in a society not conducive to or appreciative of these activities, or even worse, with a toxic or unjust environment.

Conscience: The Role of the *Qalb*

Conscience is the capacity to use intelligence in morally guided ways—for good or evil. Animals make instinctive or learned decisions, but humans have an added dimension: **morals and ethics**. The human ability to make value-based decisions is what we spiritually refer to as the *Qalb*.

The *Qalb* is not a fixed state; it is dynamic, constantly in motion—like a flickering flame. Its orientation changes based on our state of mind, which can be altered by mood, environment, substances such as intoxicants, and many other factors. This is one reason why the Qur'an warns against intoxicants (Surah Al-Ma'idah 5:90–91). The *Qalb* can be influenced by self-interest or external pressures, making it a constant struggle to maintain its moral direction.

Linguistically, *qalb* implies movement or transformation. Spiritually, it refers to the changing state of conscience, which may bring one closer to or further from Allah (SWT). Like the physical heart, the conscience can be healthy or diseased. Just as an unhealthy eye fails to see clearly, or a sick brain fails to function properly, a diseased *Qalb* misinterprets situations and makes harmful choices.

A healthy conscience leads to actions that are good for the individual and society. A diseased conscience leads to harm—both personal and social. These differences manifest in our behavior: One with a healthy *Qalb* tends to be humble, truthful, and calm, while one with a diseased *Qalb* may show arrogance, jealousy, and hypocrisy. The former focuses on self-correction, the latter blames others. This inner moral state is what drives our actions—and maintaining its health is among our greatest struggles (*jihad al-akbar*).

Keeping the *Qalb* Healthy

Many things can damage the *Qalb*. But mindfulness of God in all aspects of life—*taqwa*—helps keep it healthy. Disobedience or involvement in clearly wrong activities corrupts it, regardless of one's religion.

If we imagine intellect as the engine of a vehicle, and intelligence as its capacity to travel, then the conscience—the *Qalb*—is the driver. A good driver reaches the right destination; a reckless one causes damage. Every human being, Muslim or not, has this driver.

The *Qalb* is never static. It is constantly changing and can either improve or deteriorate. Like other ailments, a diseased *Qalb* can be healed. Remembrance of Allah SWT (*dhikr*) is often cited as a key to its health, but if not accompanied by righteous actions, *dhikr* alone may not suffice. After *Iman*, the Qur'an places greatest emphasis on *amale salih* (righteous deeds). Doing good is what keeps the conscience healthy.

What then is a righteous deed? At the very least, it is something that is not wrong. Avoiding wrongdoing is the minimum standard to preserve the *Qalb*. With effort and sincerity, one can elevate their *Qalb* to a stronger, healthier state—and rise to a higher spiritual station, *insha'Allah*.

Chapter 5

The *Qalb* 102

IN THE PREVIOUS PIECE, I INTRODUCED the concept of the *Qalb*. Here, I aim to explore it little deeper. The words and messages in the Qur'an are often symbolic or metaphorical. To understand the metaphor of the *Qalb*, it is important to first consider its basic and original context.

The *qalb*—Arabic for "heart"—is a central organ in the body, constantly beating and in motion. Linguistically, *qalb* is associated with transformation and movement. The physical heart is well-protected in the chest, encased by ribs, muscles, and tissues. It acts as a powerhouse, producing the energy needed to distribute oxygen and nutrients to every part of the body. Without this function, the body cannot survive. The heart also supports muscle function and powers all physical activity. If the heart fails, as during a heart attack, the body begins to shut down within moments.

Despite its vital role, the heart is not the master organ of the body—the brain is. The brain generates ideas, processes information, and directs bodily functions. It maintains both direct and indirect control over the heart. Yet these two organs are interdependent: The brain controls the heart's activity, and the heart supplies the blood that sustains the brain. One cannot survive without the other.

In Islamic literature, the term *Qalb* refers to what may be best translated as the "spiritual heart" or "conscience," although neither term fully captures its meaning. Like the physical heart, the *Qalb* is in constant motion—shifting, transforming, responding. But it is not a physical structure. Its "power" is not physical either: it is rather intellectual or spiritual. If the physical heart gives us strength to act, the *Qalb* governs whether those actions are worthy or not.

The foundation of the *Qalb* lies in intellect and intelligence, not emotions—though emotions strongly influence it, positively or negatively. Just as a healthy physical heart gives physical strength, a healthy *Qalb* grants moral clarity, boldness and courage. When sound, it promotes truth, fairness, and justice, encouraging virtues like generosity, forgiveness, and mercy. When diseased, it distorts perception and fosters falsehood, envy, and dishonesty—leading to traits like revenge, vengeance, and cruelty. One path leads to *ihsan* (excellence – loosely translated) and ultimate success, and the other to *zulm* (injustice – also loosely translated) and moral ruin.

Understanding the relationship between the *Qalb* and intelligence is crucial. Many misunderstand the *Qalb* as something emotional rather than intellectual. But its role mirrors that of the physical heart in relation to the brain. Intelligence provides the ability to plan or act; the *Qalb* determines whether one should act at all. A healthy *Qalb* allows for accurate perception and sound moral judgment. A diseased *Qalb* results in distortion and flawed choices, regardless of one's intellectual ability.

The *Qalb* and intelligence are interdependent. A person with strong intelligence but a diseased *Qalb* may use that intellect for harm, while a person with a virtuous *Qalb* but limited intellect may lack the tools to act effectively. The most blessed is one whose intelligence and *Qalb* are both healthy and rightly guided.

Just as the *Qalb* has a symbolic parallel in the physical heart, there is also a symbolic "chest"—the *Sadr*. As the physical chest protects the heart, the *Sadr* protects the

Qalb, the spiritual heart. A strong and sound *Sadr* supports a healthy *Qalb*. Like the skeletal rib cage, the foundation of a strong *Sadr* is *Iman* (Faith)—a proper understanding of God, the Most-praiseworthy, and our role in the larger scheme of creation. Being constantly aware or conscious of this situation, *taqwa*, is its circulatory system that provides spiritual nutrients. Deeds or character acts like the muscles—defining its strength and function, weak or strong, diseased or healthy. We all carry this spiritual apparatus. Some were born with an inherently healthy and special *Sadr* and *Qalb*, like the Prophets of Allah SWT. Many others are also blessed with somewhat similar traits. Most of us struggle to maintain a strong *Sadr* and thus a healthy *Qalb*. In this struggle, lapses, or minor wrong deeds or actions may weaken or sicken the *Qalb*. Time and opportunities are granted to amend ways and recuperate the *Qalb*. If not, or in case of major wrong actions, its fate may be sealed, keeping it permanently diseased.

Words matter—what we say, write, and share shapes us—but nothing strengthens the *Sadr*, and indirectly the *Qalb*, more than righteous deeds. Conversely, wrongful acts, even if performed by someone with belief and regularities of religious practice, may leave the *Qalb* diseased. *Dhikr* (remembrance of Allah SWT) is often recommended to stabilize the *Qalb* and prevent it from straying, and it certainly has value. However, real healing and guidance come through action—specifically, through righteous deeds. And Allah (SWT) knows best.

Selected Qur'anic References:

> *"In their hearts is disease, so Allah has increased their disease; and for them is a painful punishment because they [habitually] used to lie."* (Al-Baqarah 2:10)
>
> *"Allah has set a seal upon their hearts and upon their hearing, and over their vision is a veil…"* (Al-Baqarah 2:7)
>
> *"Our Lord, do not let our hearts deviate after You have guided us…"* (Aal Imran 3:8)
>
> *"Indeed, in the remembrance of Allah do hearts find satisfaction."* (Ar-Ra'd 13:28)
>
> *"Those who believe and do righteous deeds—for them is every blessing and a beautiful final return."* (Ar-Ra'd 13:29)
>
> *"Have you seen him who takes his own desires as his god?..."* (Al-Jathiyah 45:23)
>
> *"Those who believe and do righteous deeds—We shall blot out their evil and reward them for the best of their actions."* (Al-Ankabut 29:7)

"They prefer to stay behind. Their hearts are sealed, so they understand not." (At-Tawbah 9:87)

"Allah has sealed their hearts; so they do not know." (At-Tawbah 9:93)

"But the heart of the mother of Moses became void. Had We not strengthened her heart…" (Al-Qasas 28:10)

"Have We not expanded your chest?" (Ash-Sharh 94:1) *(Note: The word "breast" here should be understood as "chest"—as commonly translated in Urdu)*

Selected Hadith:

"Truly, in the body is a piece of flesh which, if sound, the whole body is sound, and if corrupt, the whole body is corrupt. Verily, it is the heart." (Ṣaḥīḥ al-Bukhārī 52)

"The best of people is one whose heart is pure and whose speech is sincere…" (Sunan Ibn Majah 4216)

"O Turner of hearts, make my heart firm upon Your religion." (Jami` at-Tirmidhi 3522)

"If you want to soften your heart, feed the poor and pat the head of the orphan." (Musnad Aḥmad 7576)

"One who holds nothing of the Qur'an in his heart is like a ruined house." (Sunan al-Tirmidhī 2913)

Chapter 6

The *Nafs*

IN A GATHERING WITH FRIENDS, I asked about their understanding of the Arabic word *nafs* as it appears in the Qur'an and in Islamic discourse. Unsurprisingly, there were many responses but no consensus. This reflected a broader lack of clarity surrounding the concept. Broadly speaking, *nafs* may be described as a person's psychological capacity or psychological state. As I have noted before, many Qur'anic terms—such as *riba* or *khamr*—are difficult to translate into a single English word. Attempting to do so often limits their intended meaning or creates misunderstanding.

Among well-respected Qur'an translators, *nafs* has been rendered in various ways: *my own self, the (human) soul,*

soul, inner self, myself, or *self.* Linguistically, one may also add other related meanings: spirit, psyche, mind, human being, person, individual, being, essence, or nature. Some translators choose to retain the word *nafs* untranslated, offering a separate explanation instead. I believe this is a better practice, because clarity is important when the same root-word is used for different meanings based upon its context. This practice, polysemy, at times difficult to tease out is a hallmark of good quality literary work, purposefully done to create semantic ambiguity. And the Qur'an is a Masterpiece in Arabic literature.

Usual translation of *nafs*, in the manner it is done, creates lack of clarity and confusion. For example, in the following *ayat:*

Al-Quran 3:185 "Every soul will taste death,"

Al-Quran 4:1 "O humanity! Be mindful of your Lord Who created you from a single soul,"

Compare these two *ayat* with the following:

Al-Qur'an 12:53 "And I do not seek to free myself from blame, for indeed the soul is ever inclined to evil, except those shown mercy by my Lord."

In these *ayat,* the word *nafs* is used to convey different meanings though the translator has used the same English word, "soul". In 3:185, it is about everything, at least every living thing, which will experience death. In 4:1, the subject is human beings, who started from a common ancestor. In 12:53, it means something different from the above two *ayat*. In fact, in this ayah, *nafs* is used in both ways, first, as a person and then with a different meaning, and that meaning is the topic of this writing.

Nafs may be understood as the psychological or spiritual manifestation of our physical and mental state. Like the *Qalb*, it is a spiritual concept, and the two are closely related and interactive. By analogy, the *nafs* is like the soil in which crops grow—crops of righteousness or wrongdoing—while the *Qalb* is the farmer who decides what to sow. In this sense, the *Qalb*, or conscience, is the driver of moral choice, while the *nafs* represents the psychological capacity that allows such behavior to manifest.

Just as land may grow certain plants even without deliberate cultivation, the *nafs* is influenced by the *Qalb* but does not fall entirely under its control. Its primary drive is the pursuit of physical or spiritual pleasure. However, for any meaningful "crop" to emerge, the farmer—the *Qalb*—must be involved.

Some people describe *nafs* exclusively in negative terms. This view, however, does not align with its Qur'anic usage, where *nafs* is also described in the most elevated and praiseworthy manner. For example:

Al-Qur'an 89:27–28 "O tranquil soul! Return to your Lord, well pleased ⌜with Him⌝ and well pleasing ⌜to Him⌝."

Seeking or desiring for pleasure is a powerful and fundamental human instinct. Experiencing pleasure is not inherently harmful; rather, it is essential for physical survival and spiritual well-being. Even some less pleasurable experiences serve protective psychological and immune functions. On a spiritual level, waking up in the wee hours to pray is physically burdensome but has a value of its own. However, experiences that are excessively unpleasant may cause lasting harm, such as psychological trauma.

A newborn, for example, instinctively seeks milk because hunger is unpleasant and feeding is pleasurable. Similarly, a hungry person eats because eating brings pleasure, and tastier food brings even greater pleasure. At a basic level, physical pleasure is mediated through the senses—smell, touch, taste, hearing, and sight—while spiritual pleasure arises from thoughts, psychological feelings, and emotions.

The *nafs* can be partially or fully governed by the pursuit of pleasure. In such a state, it may resist external guidance or rational restraint and follow only its own desires. Whether this results in benefit or harm depends on the nature of the pleasure being pursued. Some people equivalate *nafs* to desire, but desire or the pursuit is only a process, or a mean to reach what *nafs* is really looking for.

It is relatively easy to recognize negative aspects of physical pleasure, though not all physical pleasure is harmful, only when it crosses a line or disturbs brain's equilibrium. Even before one may consider personal context, any pleasure that harms any other being is crossing that line. Spiritual pleasures are no different; they too can become destructive. A powerful example of spiritual pleasure is a mother's love for her child. While this love is deeply noble, it can become harmful if misguided or excessive, potentially impairing the child's well-being. Power, social or political, with its multiple dimensions and ways to assert, is commonly desired and frequently abused. Pleasure of any type of realistic or assumed power can be easily addictive and destructive. Other examples of sources of spiritual pleasure people may derive are irrational ideologies or harmful practices.

Although humans share biological traits with animals, they differ in important ways. Animals eat when hungry; humans may eat even when they are not hungry and may eat purely for enjoyment. In such cases, the *nafs* becomes dominated by the pleasure of consumption. In extreme forms, this may manifest as pathological behavior, such as binge eating followed by purging. Similar patterns can be observed with other forms of physical pleasure.

At a deeper level, pleasure has a biological basis. Pleasure signals are processed in two major brain systems: the deep mesolimbic system and many higher cortical regions, particularly the frontal and parietal lobes, and the insular cortex. Animals possess the mesolimbic system, but humans are endowed with more developed higher cortical structures. These additional brain regions enable more complex forms of pleasure-seeking. Without restraint on the *nafs*, and aided by this complex neurobiology, humans may pursue limitless and increasingly intense forms of pleasure.

The brain, however, seeks homeostasis—balance and moderation. Excessive pleasure, even when biologically reinforced, can be detrimental. When Allah (SWT) instructs us to reform ourselves, it is for our own benefit:

Al-Qur'an 17:15 "Whoever chooses guidance, it is only for their own good; and whoever chooses to stray, it is only to their own loss."

Al-Qur'an 41:46 "Whoever does good, it is to their own benefit; and whoever does evil, it is to their own loss."

Among all human pleasures, sexual intimacy is perhaps the most intense. As indicated in the Qur'an, 30:21 and 17:32, it carries both profound reward and profound risk, depending how it is managed. Its association to *nafs* is exemplified in the following *ayah*:

Al-Qur'an 12:53 "And I do not seek to free myself from blame, for indeed the soul is ever inclined to evil, except those shown mercy by my Lord."

This verse is among the most frequently cited when scholars discuss the concept of *nafs*. It occurs within the story of Prophet Yusuf (Joseph) (AS), peace be upon him. After Yusuf (AS) interpreted the king's dream, he was invited to leave prison but insisted that his name first be cleared of the false accusation of an affair made against him years earlier. The king questioned the women involved, including the wife of the minister, the perpetrator of the whole affair, who admitted her wrongdoing and absolved Yusuf (AS) completely.

A scholarly question arises: who uttered these words—Yusuf or the minister's wife? The Qur'an does not explicitly clarify this. While many scholars attribute them to him, others attribute them to the woman herself, which seems to be the case if one also reads an *ayah* before it.

The opening phrase of this *ayah*, *"I do not seek to free myself from blame,"* suggests acceptance of responsibility, which seems more consistent with the woman's position. The statement that *"the soul is ever inclined to evil"* is a universal truth and applies regardless of the speaker.

If these words are attributed to the woman, they reflect remarkable moral clarity. She acknowledges her fault, recognizes the power of the *nafs*, clears Yusuf's name, and corrects her own psychological and spiritual state. In doing so, she acts in a manner pleasing to Allah (SWT).

Any reflective person, granted special mercy from Allah (SWT), may resist wrongful temptation and restrain their *nafs*. If erred, like the minister's wife, they may feel guilty. Such individuals are blessed, as indicated by the following *ayah*:

Al-Qur'an 75:2 "And I swear by the self-reproaching soul."

Self-reproach or guilt is not entirely bad; it is the key to self-correction. This is a never-ending process and there is always room for spiritual growth and closeness to Allah. The key lies in controlling the *nafs*—not eliminating it but regulating its pursuit of pleasure. The Prophet Muhammad (SAW) exemplified this balance, enjoying permissible pleasures of life while attaining the highest spiritual rank.

As with the *Qalb*, the *nafs* is not static. It is in constant flux and is influenced by biological and mental states. As a child matures into adolescence and adulthood, the *nafs* evolves, particularly as cognitive and analytical abilities develop. Hormonal changes and their indirect impact on the brain plays a strong part. Cultural, social and political factors also impact its state. Self-analysis and self-rebuke are key components of righteous behavior or the "middle-path" (*siraatay mustaqeem*). This may lead to a revived state of an individual's *Qalb*, which may positively impact their *nafs*. This state of *nafs* with feelings of guilt is specially recognized and exemplified in the above ayah.

Scholars usually describe different aspects of *nafs* as follows: *Ammarah* (desire-driven), *lawwamah* (self-critical), and *mutmainnah* (tranquil). Some go even further, describing it *mulhimah* (inspired), *radiyah* (content), *mardiyyah* (divinely pleasing), and *kamilah* (complete). A person's *nafs* may go through some or all these stages at different times. A *nafs* that is fully *mutmain* or tranquil is description of a *nafs* in the hereafter declared successful, which is the ultimate success. In this life, we may have its experience but to a varying degree. It is like the relation of sleep with death; in sleep, we are exposed to a death-like state every day, but death itself is ultimate and different. Our *nafs* may be tranquil at different times of our life but ultimate and full tranquility is only if we succeed in the hereafter.

Nafs-al-ammarah is also a part of our makeup. There are people whose life is all but pleasure and desire-driven, as they are consumed by this aspect of their *nafs*. Most of us though are in the middle, trying to analyze and critique our words and actions. Some do it little, and some are constantly involved in this analysis. If done right, we assume a feeling of guilt, some may get it more and some less. This guilt is a blessing. Anyone without this guilt may have a larger problem. This guilt may become the basis to take corrective actions, if, like the wife of the minister in the story of Yusuf (AS), we change our *Qalb*, accept responsibility of our wrong actions and fulfill accountability.

Striving against the temptations of one's own *nafs* is rarely easy. Confronting an external enemy that one can see or understand may be far simpler than struggling against an adversary that is internal and not fully perceived. In this context, the Prophet (SAW) is reported to have said:

"The *mujahid* is the one who strives against his
own *nafs* for the sake of Allah."
Sunan al-Tirmidhi.

A person may succeed in restraining certain desires or resisting temptations by not acting upon them. With regard to involuntary thoughts or inner whispers, there is divine leniency so long as they are neither acted upon nor verbalized:

"Allah has forgiven my ummah for what their *nafs* whispers to them, as long as they do not act upon it or speak of it."
Ṣaḥih al-Bukhari (5269, 6664).

We are all born with a particular psychological disposition, or *nafs*, which can incline us toward either right or wrong behavior. This disposition differs from person to person. For both personal and societal well-being, it is essential to recognize the destructive potential of the *nafs* and to have mechanisms in place to keep it in check. For some, this may be relatively easy; for most—me included—it is a formidable and ongoing struggle. Nevertheless, we must persist in this effort and strive to subdue our *nafs*, as the Prophet (SAW) said:

"The intelligent one is the one who subdues his *nafs* and works for what comes after death…" *Sunan al-Tirmidhi* (2459).

Establishing practical mechanisms to restrain the *nafs*—a subject worthy of its own discussion and one that may differ for everyone—can be guided by certain foundational principles. Among them are the following Qur'anic reminders:

Al-Qur'an 96:14 "Does he not know that Allah sees?"

A constant awareness of Allah's presence restrains the *nafs* more effectively than fear alone.

Al-Qur'an 17:36 "Do not follow that of which you have no knowledge."

This guidance is especially relevant in an age saturated with messages from every direction, many of which arrive cloaked in moral, ethical, or even religious language.

May Allah (SWT) include us among those whose *nafs* is inclined toward goodness, those who remain conscious and uneasy when it begins to drift downward and always have a mechanism in place to correct its expression. Amin.

Chapter 7

The Matter of the *Hijri* Calendar

An example of a deeper problem

ALMOST 1400 YEARS AGO, the last Prophet or the official Messenger of Allah (translated as God in English) (*Subhana wa Ta'aala* - Glorified and Exalted), died. May Allah (SWT) raise his ranks even further and bless his family, his community, and his followers forever to come. Amen. This event, though clearly not unusual, shocked some of his followers. Some, to the extent of refusing to accept the reality. But thanks to Abu Bakr, Prophet's closest companion, may Allah SWT be please with him, stood up and addressed the community and provided a logical analysis of the event. He stated:

"Whoever amongst you worshipped Muhammad, then Muhammad is dead, but whoever worshipped Allah, Allah is alive and will never die. Allah said: 'Muhammad is no more than an Apostle and indeed (many) Apostles have passed away before him ...' (Al-Quran 3:144)".

This was an incredibly courageous, astute, and significant speech from an otherwise humble and soft-hearted man. Abu Bakr (RA) was not talking about worshipping the Prophet as we worship Allah (SWT). He was talking about irrational or illogical thinking and behavior about the Prophet, his actions, and his personality. At the same time, he was reminding everyone about Allah (SWT), by directly mentioning His words, the Qur'an, the everlasting source of information, knowledge, and wisdom. Since then, people like to believe that Abu Bakr (RA) permanently resolved this issue but a little reflection on Muslim situation easily tell us that the issue never completely disappeared. In later generations, unchecked and actively promoted by some religious establishment, it thrived in many Muslim communities and is especially rampant in the Indian sub-continent.

1st Reminder: The Qur'an is the primary source of information and guidance, confirmed by the Prophet

Muhammad (SAW) himself. Value of the Qur'an is like the constitution providing unbreakable fundamental principles though not all rules and regulations. Rules & regulations are designed based upon its principles. In addition, guidance is obtained from the *Hadith* and the *Sunnah* (speech and conduct of the Prophet SAW) available to us as documented historical records.

Certain aspect of religion like what is required to be a Muslim, how to pray *salat*, how many times to pray, when and how to fast, how much to pay for *Zakat*, or the details of the *Hajj* are well defined and are performed as the Prophet (SAW) did or recommended. Principles about them are in the Qur'an and details in the *Hadith*. A lot of other matters are of different nature, like how to determine the time of *salat*, calculate *Zakat* on a stock portfolio, or when a new *Hijri* month starts. For such matters, the Prophet (SAW) and the early generations used their means and tools, which now are either obsolete or inappropriate, not because they were wrong but because better and more accurate means are available, as I discuss it further.

2nd Reminder: Illogical and false understanding of a concept always ends up in illogical and false conclusion, and religion is not an exception to this rule. There are examples in the Qur'an to make this point.

Now let's look at the *Hijri* calendar, which is a lunar calendar. But before I do that, for someone not aware of planetary system, which provides the basis for daily and yearly calendars, it is important to review some basic astronomy:

1. Earth is a rounded planet, not flat, and it is constantly moving in two different ways. It moves around the sun at a speed of 67,000 miles per hour. It is also moving around its own body or its own axis, like a spinning top, at about 1,000 miles per hour. This movement of earth on its axis gives us days and nights. The side of earth facing the sun has the day and the other side has the night, while one whole rotation takes a day. The concept of dividing the day in 24-hours is ancient but the clock showing 12 hours that we use today, to figure out and announce times of daily salat is only a few hundred years old. Before that, people used many other though not as reliable or precise methods to figure out time of the day, such as visibly following the sun's movement in the sky during daytime and movement of stars at night, sundial (following the shadow of a stick in the ground), a water clock (elaborate water containers with holes), or hourglasses with sand. Ancient Chinese, Egyptians, and Babylon's, they all had similar contraptions to determine time of

the day. The first generation of Muslims probably used the method of visibly observing the location of the sun and the stars or the sundial method to determine salat timings.

2. Movement of earth around the sun gives us the year because it takes about 365 days for earth to finish this rotation. Concept of how seasons come about is little more complicated and not addressed here.

3. Moon is rotating around the earth, and together they are rotating around the sun. The Moon does not have its own light, and it is not shining on its own. It becomes visible to us through the reflected sunlight from its surface, which is different from the Sun (Ref: Al-Quran, 10:5). We may see the whole of the Sun with its own light every day but not of the Moon, which is visible only through the reflected light. As the Moon itself is circling around the Earth, it becomes less visible when it reaches where the sunlight going in its direction is blocked by the Earth, and we only see a part of it, which is the basis of the so-called moon phases. (This phenomenon is better understood with pictures, which are available online). It takes 29.5 days for the moon phases that we see to repeat.

4. Concept of lunar calendar, or a calendar based upon observing the phases of the Moon, is very old. Almost every ancient civilization relied on moon phases to figure out their calendars. A lunar calendar year is always a few days shorter than the solar calendar or the conventional calendar we follow. To avoid too many fluctuations in dates and seasons, different people used different methods and adjusted their calendars. Usually, a month was added at periodic intervals, like the Jewish calendar. *Hijri* calendar that started at the time of the Prophet's migration to Medina, or *Hijra*, is a lunar calendar based upon lunar phases and it does not make any such correction. This is the reason that *Ramadan* comes a few days earlier every year than the previous year.

5. Movements of the Earth, the Moon, and the Sun are precise and predictable, not a fraction less or a fraction more than what the system is designed for. If that would happen, the whole system could collapse, which was the reason Allah SWT challenged us (Ref: Al-Quran, 67:3-4) to reflect on this flawless system. Just like a modern clock can figure out time of the day to the fraction of a second, with the sophistication and knowledge

available to us today, we can precisely figure out when and where the Moon and the Earth are going to be at any future date, including the moon phases. The system is perfect if we only pay attention to it and try to use it to make a calendar as Allah SWT recommended in the Quran:

Al-Quran, *6*:96 "At the crack of dawn, He causes the morning to emerge. He made the night still, and He rendered the sun and the moon to serve as calculation devices. Such is the design of the Almighty, the Omniscient."

Al-Quran, 10:5 "HE is the One who has made the sun radiant and the moon a light and measured out for it 'heavenly' mansions 'through which it traverses', so that you may know the number of the years and 'their' calculation. God did not create 'all' this, except with 'the very essence of' truth. He makes distinct the signs 'in creation' for a people who 'would reflect on them and' know 'God'".

Islam, as clearly stated in the Qur'an, promotes logical thinking. There are numerous explicit scientific facts and principles mentioned in the Qur'an, including the above to guide us to the right path, or a better path. For centuries, Muslims were not averse to logical thinking and analysis, or what we usually call science, and applying it to their day-to-day life. A lot of present-day Muslims are like that too. But a lot many, especially a large section of the religious establishment is not.

When it comes to making the *Hijri* calendar, in one way or another, we insist on visibly seeing the Moon. Wearing eyeglasses and even a telescope is allowed, so science is not completely thrown out, like the breast of the chicken is *halal* and the rest is *haram*, and the insistence is on seeing the Moon. This means that there is something compulsory and holy, like an act of worship, about seeing the Moon. But moon sighting is just a method to observe a natural phenomenon, or a tool to follow its phases. It is no different from, in old times, going out and seeing the shadow of a stick in the ground, or even the position of the Sun in the horizon to see if it was the time for *Asr salat* or not. Moonsighting has been made an essential or compulsory ritual with the argument, even if it is done by a few, that the Prophet SAW did it. But the Prophet and the first generation did a lot many things that we now do not consider doing, like for example finding the *salat* timing with the shadow of a stick in the ground. This issue is so pervasive and so much emphasized that some Muslim countries have a whole bureaucracy of religious scholars to find the Moon every month! To make things worse, similar institutions have been created in non-Muslim societies like the USA. If UN was in Muslim's hands, they would likely create a global bureaucracy of the so-called religious scholars to find the Moon every month. This is absurd to say the least, and a clear example of the Prophet worshipping Abu Bakr (RA) rejected and warned us about.

Trying to see the Moon was fine when no better option was available but after human society evolved to where we are now, we cannot defend having the same policy. It is like saying that we would continue to use sundial or hourglasses instead of modern time pieces.

The principle and the tools to use for establishing the time of the day and the calendar was stated in the above-mentioned *ayah* of the Qur'an. The Qur'an provided an explanation and approach, which humans later found to be true and logical. The Prophet (SAW) followed the Qur'anic principle and used it in the manner he could. But our problem is that we do not want to accept what is written in the Qur'an, about which the Qur'an also stated:

Al-Qur'an *25:30* "Then the Messenger will say: "O my Lord! Truly my people took this Qur'an for just foolish nonsense.""

Only looking at the most superficial of meanings, we conveniently explain to ourselves that "my people" here is not us, it was only the Quraysh of Mecca! We deceive ourselves in so many ways. (I covered the issue of, "how to interpret a Qur'anic *ayah?*", in a separate chapter.)

3rd Reminder: Human society is evolving and slowly getting increasingly sophisticated or knowledgeable, fair, and just. This statement may seem incorrect to some depending upon a time-period of history or a specific issue, but it becomes abundantly clear with a deeper and unbiased reflection upon history. It is illogical and wrong to take it back. It will not happen, and if tried, it will only slow us down or make us irrelevant. People who insist on less sophistication or less knowledge, in a way, are also insisting on less fairness and less justice.

In the matter of a calendar, many people do not pay attention to the impact of insistence on less sophistication. The world now is very interconnected and relies on way more predictability and advanced scheduling compared to the early generations of Muslims. The issue of *Hijri* calendar is a prime example of Muslim's lack of respect for such critical concepts and the concept of time. Due to its unpredictability, institutions, airlines, or doctor offices are unable to guarantee their schedules. In the USA, the system allows a Muslim to take a day off for religious observance, whatever that day is. The problem is that a Muslim employee can never reliably tell his employer when that day is going to be. Impact of unpredictable *Hijri* calendar is either completely ignored or frequently disregarded, and sometimes even praised. Ignoring the fact that it creates undue frustration, stress, loss of people's time, and could very well cause physical and financial harm due to delayed or cancelled services. For our present times, it is unfair and unjust and is only happening because of religious establishment's insistence on less sophistication.

With the level of present-day astronomical understanding, and the resources available to us, the policy of the so-called "local" or "global" moonsighting do not follow the full message of the Qur'an and the spirit of Islam. It is dogmatic based upon either a fear of not following a *hadith*, or an irrational sense of righteousness. We must follow the instructions in the Qur'an and understand the underlying principle of this issue. There is an acute need to formulate a precise lunar calendar based upon moon's phases, in advance, and standardized across the globe. May Allah SWT guide us to the right path, Amen.

Chapter 8

Sectarianism

The curse of the superiority complex

SECTARIANISM, IN THE OXFORD ENGLISH Dictionary, is defined as, "excessive attachment to a particular sect or party, especially in religion". Its negative impact on the society is same both in religious and political spheres. It promotes extremism and zero-sum way of thinking. It may also be defined as a narrow-minded adherence to a particular sect, often leading to conflict with people differing in opinion. There are references in the Bible against this concept and in the Qur'an. Despite that, these divine instructions are commonly ignored by both Christians and the Muslims, especially their leaders. Fundamental reasons for this behavior, in my opinion, is less to do with theological epiphany of the promotors but rather more for the material or egotistical benefit they accrue. Human ego at times can be as devastating as the energy of a wild animal in rut, who could fight to death to gain an upper hand.

It is deeply painful to witness individuals arguing to prove their superiority over others or attempting to outmaneuver them. Interpretations of the *ayat* of the Qur'an, or the selective acceptance or rejection of certain *hadiths* or their interpretations are the tools, or rather the weapons, they employ. Such attitudes and practices contradict the clear guidance given by Allah (SWT) in the Qur'an. The Qur'an explicitly warns against division and urges believers to unite:

Al-Qur'an 3:103 "*And hold firmly to the rope of Allah all together, and do not become divided. And remember the favor of Allah upon you...*"

Al-Qur'an 6:159 "*Indeed, you 'O Prophet' are not responsible whatsoever for those who have divided their faith and split into sects. Their judgement rest only with Allah. And He will inform them of what they use to do.*"

Aside from divisions within the Muslim community, the Qur'an also provides unequivocal instructions about people who may not agree with their ideology:

Al-Qur'an 2:256 "*Let there be no compulsion in religion, for the truth stands out clearly from falsehood. So whoever renounces false gods and believes in Allah has certainly grasped the firmest, unfailing handhold. And Allah is All-Hearing, All-Knowing.*"

Al-Qur'an 109:6 "*To you be your Way, and to me mine.*"

Al-Qur'an 49:13 "*O humanity! Indeed, We created you from a male and a female and made you into peoples and tribes so that you may 'get to' know one another. Surely the most noble of you in the sight of Allah is the most righteous among you. Allah is truly All-Knowing, All-Aware.*"

Despite such unequivocal guidance, many in the so-called Muslim countries identify themselves by the sect of their forefathers or personal choosing. Institutions and communities often perpetuate this thinking, labeling mosques or organizations with sectarian identities, further entrenching this type of division. This behavior blatantly contradicts Qur'anic teachings.

Sadly, even respected scholars—often revered by their followers—have, at times, promoted sectarian superiority in their writings or statements. The pervasive nature of this issue has led many to overlook the broader unifying message of Islam in favor of factional pride. People do not understand that when a scholar in his speech or writing describes and promotes an opinion as the opinion of "*ahlay Sunnah*" or "*ahlay Bait*", he or she is promoting sectarianism. One may easily find this anomaly in the writings of many past scholars who are frequently quoted in the sermons and speeches.

In some places though, like for example in Pakistan, the state itself has become the promotor of this practice with help of its Ministry of Religious Affairs, which has only helped to institutionalize these practices. On a surface level, this type of differentiation may seem benign and a natural evolution of "freedom of religious practices." Looking closely though, as its basis is rooted in self-righteousness, rejection of the alternate and above all material gains, it has resulted in intolerance, extremism, and lawlessness. Even in best of circumstances, financial fraud and abuses related to these practices mostly remain unchecked.

The Qur'an makes it abundantly clear that division is not part of Allah's design for the Muslim *ummah*. We must, individually and collectively reject sectarianism in all forms—whether through speech, actions, or institutional affiliations. No action should be taken that directly or indirectly promotes sectarian identity or thinking.

The practice of labeling a mosque or institution with a sect or school of thought stands in direct contradiction to the Qur'an's call for unity. As Muslims, we are instructed to hold fast to the "rope of Allah," embracing the unity of faith and rejecting all forms of division. We must not ignore speech and writings, no matter by who, that directly or indirectly promote this practice. We must stay away from any material or financial gain accrued from establishing or promoting an opinion or a practice. May Allah SWT guide us to the right path, but that path may not be in our reach if we do not first make changes in our practices and behaviors.

Chapter 9

The Human Slavery

THERE ARE SOME IMPORTANT TOPICS, especially social behaviors and their basis, one may seldom hear in a *Jumah Khutba* or otherwise in a masjid setting. Slavery is one of them and the reasons for this omission are manifold. On the other hand, understanding of this issue is fundamental to have a grasp of many major social and political issues, not just in the United States of America but all over the world. While ancestors of significant part of American Muslims experienced enslavement and might have easier time understanding its impact, most present-day Muslims do not have any such history or an emotional connection to this subject. As a result, most do not fully understand its practical, social, and emotional implications. This subject is quite vast and mostly only one aspect is discussed here, its Islamic religious injunction.

Slavery in its extreme form implied complete ownership of a person—man, woman, or a child—by another individual or a governing authority, akin to owning a bicycle or a home. This ownership granted the master the ability to use the enslaved person in any manner desired, often depriving them of rights and subjecting them to harm, sale, or exchange at the owner's whim. Different societies tried to provide some type of legal framework to avoid conflicts and abuse, but that did not change the basic premise of ownership.

The institution of slavery dates to the earliest recorded human history, including mentions in the Sumerian records (3100 BCE) and the records of later ancient civilizations. Slavery was a worldwide phenomenon. Racial differences were a significant factor in enslavement, as seen in ancient Egypt and the recent history of the United States. However, other prevalent reasons included war (prisoners of war), debt (exploitative lending practices), political persecutions, and criminal punishment. Before the Prophethood of Muhammad (SAW), slavery was an established institution in Mecca and Arabia, governed by a set of traditions that permitted the ownership and trade of human beings.

It is widely understood that neither the Qur'an nor the Prophet Muhammad (SAW) explicitly prohibited slavery in the manner that the consumption of swine is prohibited. However, the Qur'an contains references to slavery, and the *Hadith* literature extensively discuss its ethics. While the *Hadith* literature primarily focuses on the humane treatment of slaves, the Qur'an actively promotes emancipation and encourages kind and generous treatment of those under one's authority. The Prophet Muhammad (SAW), through both his actions and statements, exemplified this conduct. According to some reports, the Prophet (SAW) was raising concern about women and slaves, while he was terminally ill, like there was some unfinished business he needed to attend to. Despite this, slavery persisted in Muslim societies until modern history. Haiti became the first nation to abolish slavery in 1804. The United States did it in 1865, Saudi Arabia in 1962, and finally Mauritania in 1981.

At present time, the topic of slavery is a complex and equally painful for both parties, for those whose ancestors were enslaved and the descendants of the slave owners. For Muslims, it also presents a theological challenge: how to reconcile the Qur'an, the *Hadith*, and the practices of the early generations with the now universally accepted view that slavery is immoral and illegal. However, this challenge also provides an opportunity for deep reflection and the re-examination of historical practices in the light of Islamic teachings.

There are matters of belief, such as *Tawheed* (the oneness of God), the Prophethood of Muhammad (SAW), and the Hereafter, which remain between the individual and Allah (SWT). However, practical matters are different and can be divided into two types: those that primarily concern the individual's relationship with Allah (such as prayer, fasting, and Hajj) and those that impact other individuals (such as financial transactions, inheritance, the *Hijri* calendar, war, and the practice of slavery). Islamic teachings provide guidance on all these matters, and some degree of flexibility is inherent in all religious acts beyond the core tenets of faith.

Many Muslims believe that the early generations of Muslims had the best understanding of Islam, the Qur'an, and the *Hadith*. For some, any challenge to this notion is seen as heretical. However, the Prophet Muhammad (SAW) himself stated in his famous sermon at Mt. Arafat that later generations might develop a better understanding of his message. Historical evidence suggests that slavery remained an established practice in Muslim societies and its abolition was not prioritized. Islamic literature contains numerous references about ethics of slavery, which serves as proof of its continued presence in previous

Muslim societies. To those who argue that no religious understanding of the early generations can be challenged, I pose this question: If given the opportunity, should we re-establish the institution of slavery? If yes; why and we have a larger problem, and if not; why not? Reflecting on this question may lead to a deeper understanding of the Qur'an and the *Hadith* and help resolve this matter and many other similar issues. I believe, not addressing this matter is one of the main reasons, in Muslim societies, for not addressing and stopping many injustices, including the modern-day practice of slavery.

From an Islamic perspective, the most important information about this subject is in the Qur'an, a few verses of Surah **Al-Balad (90:8-13**), translated as follows:

"Have We not made for him a pair of eyes? And a tongue, and a pair of lips? And shown him the two highways? But he hath made no haste on the path that is steep. And what will explain to thee the path that is steep? (It is:) freeing the bondman." (Translated by Abdullah Yusuf Ali)

"Have We not given them two eyes, A tongue, and two lips; And shown them the two ways of right and wrong? If only they had attempted the challenging path of goodness instead! And what will make you realize what attempting the challenging path is? It is to free a slave." (Translated by Dr. Mustafa Khattab)

Deciphering These Lines

The reference to the eyes in the verse, "Have We not given them two eyes?" is not merely a reminder of God's favor in granting two eye-globes or the sight. It is highlighting people's indifference to the injustice and cruelty unfolding openly before them. This rhetorical question carries a meaning akin to someone pointing out an obvious reality—like when we stumble upon something apparent in a room, and someone asks, "Don't you have eyes?" In this context, the verse challenges us to recognize injustices that we witness and not turn a blind eye to them. Our gift of sight is not simply for personal benefit but also imposes a moral responsibility to observe, acknowledge, and respond to wrongdoing in our surroundings.

Similarly, the next line, "A tongue and two lips," is not just a reminder of the blessing of having these organs or our ability to speak. It is indicating to people's silence against overt injustice. It is as if someone asks, if we remain silent when we may have talked and help stop injustice: "Don't you have tongue?" This verse urges us to use our speech to advocate for what is right and to speak out against wrongs, rather than remaining passive or indifferent. Just as seeing wrongdoing obligates us to acknowledge it, being given the power of speech holds us accountable for raising our voices in the face of injustice and oppression.

The following two lines present two possible paths or courses of action: one that is easy but incorrect, and the other that is difficult yet the right course of action. Allegorically, the difficult path is described as a narrow alley and anyone traveling through risks attack from higher elevations. However, to reach the other side—one that is better in both physical and spiritual terms—one must take this arduous route. The passage then poses a provoking question: *And what will make you realize what attempting the challenging path is?"* It is like questioning someone who is witnessing ongoing injustice and cruelty but does not take the rightfully correct but difficult step of stopping it, by saying: What will it take for you to take the right step?

Finally, in the concluding verse, the steep path, the preferred course of action for the context of these *ayat* is clearly stated in just two words: *"fakku raqqaba."*

Understanding *Fakku Raqqaba*

The word *fakku* derives from *fakka*, meaning to dismantle, disassemble, take down, break apart, disengage, or free. The next word, *raqqaba*, often translated as bondman, slave or metaphorically "a neck," conveys the concept of manumission, emancipation, or ransoming—dismantling the foundation of enslavement. While these words are commonly translated as "freeing a slave," in the context of the previous verses, they carry a broader implication: Abolish slavery. And Allah SWT knows best.

The Implied vs Categorical Messaging

Some Quranic messages are categorical, like the prohibition of consuming meat of swine. Others are conveyed differently or are implied, as seen in the prohibition of alcohol or a drug like cocaine. Neither of them is mentioned in the Qur'an but the basis of their prohibition is provided. The verses of the Qur'an, 5:90-91, do not explicitly prohibit alcohol, they imply to that effect. Similarly, abolition of the institution of slavery might not be obvious in the Qur'an, but it is clearly implied. There is profound wisdom in this approach of implied messaging. For example, if, instead of the word *khmar* in the Qur'an, 5:90-91, alcohol was specifically mentioned, eating a ripe banana might have become impermissible.

The verses of Surah Al-Balad continue to remind us: *observe, reflect, speak out, and act.* The right path—the path of struggle—may seem difficult, even dangerous, but it is necessary to combat enslavement anywhere and in any form. These verses are not meant for mere recitation for blessings; they are a call to action.

Discussions of slavery can be uncomfortable for many Muslims, leading to arguments about its complexity, persistence throughout history, or claims that the Muslim approach was more humane. Some suggest that instances of slaves rising to power disprove discrimination. However, using such examples to justify or downplay slavery is flawed; the elevated status of a few does not negate the broader injustice. The fact that former slaves who gained authority were still labeled as "slaves" reveals how deeply rooted and normalized slavery was in many Muslim societies—even into modern times.

Modern day slavery comes in somewhat different form, but its impact is no less devastating. United Nations defines common form of slavery as human trafficking, forced labor, forced marriage, and debt bondage. I also add political and economic persecution in this list. Looking through this angle, human slavery is still rampant and widespread, both in Muslim or non-Muslim societies, frequently unchecked, and in some places actively promoted or institutionalized. *Ayat* of the Qur'an continue to challenge us to use our senses, raise our voices, and take concrete physical steps to stop and take down these unjust and cruel practices and policies.

The allegorical use of the steep or challenging path powerfully illustrates the moral and ethical dilemma faced by an individual or a society: the choice between the comfort of inaction and the challenge of doing what is right. The recommended path is fraught with obstacles and dangers, symbolizing the social pressures and difficulties inherent in confronting entrenched injustice. By asking, "*And what will explain to thee the path that is steep?*" The Qur'an calls upon believers to deeply reflect on the courage required to oppose wrongdoing, even when it means enduring hardship or standing alone.

Historically, one of the worst examples of human slavery was practiced in the United States of America before the Emancipation Proclamation. Individuals and local societies who took the bold and corrective path to help dismantle this system took tremendous personal and political risk. Fighting with the other side, who wanted to continue this institution, a lot of people paid a heavy price during the American Civil War. At the end though, this protracted injustice was stopped and dismantled. Subsequently, the whole society was rewarded, and the country became the de-facto leader of the world.

But the time has passed, people have forgotten certain things, and it is time to reflect on this issue again as the remnants of the old unfair ideology and other but equally abusive practices happening now, some on global scale, are asking for our attention. Examples of this are noted in governmental policies towards many residents on its soil, or its support for even worse in the Middle East. The larger society in the U. S. A, in today's post Emancipation

Proclamation standards, has adapted a wrong course again, which promotes and/or institutionalize human enslavement, locally and on international level, albeit indirectly. Just like in the case of enslavement of African Americans, a section of the religious establishment of differing faith groups, whose better job was to help chart a righteous course, is leading the society in opposite direction. The words of the Qur'an challenge these practices, and are reminding us again to open our eyes, use our speech, and take the difficult but the righteous path of fairness and justice.

For a Muslim, it is also important to approach this topic with humility and an open mindset. Re-evaluating previous interpretations of the Qur'an does not imply a lack of respect for those who preceded us. Much like younger generations may thoughtfully differ from previous ones, we can critically review historical practices and their religious foundations while maintaining due regard for past contributions. Such reflection and ongoing learning are vital for effectively addressing complex challenges facing the Muslim community and broader society.

Chapter 10

The Zakat Conundrum

AFTER ACKNOWLEDGING ALLAH SWT as the Creator and Sustainer of all physical and non-physical entities and recognizing the position of humanity in His grand design, the Qur'an repeatedly emphasize the importance of performing the righteous deeds. Concept of what the righteous deeds are is broad and I have briefly touched it while discussing the Islamic concept of the *Qalb*. In the category, establishing and performing *Salat* (prayer) and paying *Zakat* are often mentioned together. In addition, there is clear recommendation and encouragement for charitable spending, both in the conduct of the Prophet (SAW), and in the Qur'an, as illustrated in the following verse:

Al-Quran 2:177: *"Righteousness is not in turning your faces towards the east or the west. Rather, the righteous are those who believe in Allah, the Last Day, the angels, the Books, and the prophets; who give charity out of their cherished wealth to relatives, orphans, the poor, needy travelers, beggars, and for freeing captives; who establish prayer, pay alms-tax, and keep the pledges they make; and who are patient in times of suffering, adversity, and in the heat of battle. It is they who are true in faith, and it is they who are mindful of Allah."*

The verse emphasizes two types of charitable giving, both equally important. The first type is voluntary charity, which can be given at any time and in any amount. It can be given to a variety of causes while a list is provided for some preferred ones. Many people may not realize that, for a believer, alleviating poverty is as obligatory as many other articles of faith, as clearly stated in this verse. In addition, both believing in Allah and this type of charity, though obligatory for a believer, are voluntary concepts, not enforceable by an outside authority.

The second type of charity is the *Zakat*, often translated as the alms-tax. It is best understood as a religiously mandated tax calculated not on income, but on wealth that one accumulates and have possession of for at least a year. Like the charity described above, *Zakat* is obligatory but only for those who possess a certain level of wealth. It does not apply to the poor or may not apply to the lower-middle class either. Other key differences between the two types of giving are that the amount or the rate of *Zakat* is well-defined and, just like a tax, can be enforced by a governing authority. In contrast, voluntary charity is a personal matter, based upon one's conscience, a matter between the individual and Allah SWT.

Zakat becomes due only when certain assets have accumulated to a defined level and are held for at least a year. Its rate is also clearly defined. It can be disbursed to its recipients privately by its payer, or, in some situations, the governing authority may collect and use it for the welfare of the needy or deserving causes.

The recipients of *Zakat* are clarified in the following verse:

Al-Quran 9:60: "Alms-tax is only for the poor and the needy, for those employed to administer it, for those whose hearts are attracted to the faith, for freeing slaves, for those in debt, for Allah's cause, and for needy travelers. This is an obligation from Allah. And Allah is All-Knowing, All-Wise."

However, details about how much to give or the rates of *Zakat* are not explicitly mentioned in the Qur'an. This detail is derived from the *Hadith*. For those seeking more in-depth information, I recommend consulting a collection of the *Hadith*, such as **Al-Muwatta** by Imam Malik ibn Anas, may Allah SWT be pleased with him. I have also consulted other works like **Sahih Bukhari, Sahih Muslim** and **Sunan Ibn Majah** to gather a broader perspective on this topic.

While I use the term "resources" to describe the wealth on which *Zakat* may be due, this concept was not without confusion even for early Muslims. For instance, Imam Malik, may Allah (SWT) be pleased with him, expressed his opinion in **Al-Muwatta 17:1, 3** (page 230): "*Zakat* is only paid on three things: the produce of cultivated land, gold and silver, and livestock." Some may interpret this opinion lightly, but I believe it is an important reflection of the challenges faced by early Muslims as they established rules of *Zakat*.

Material resources subject to *Zakat* can be divided into three broad categories based on their nature and the level of effort required to benefit from them:

> **Type I**: Resources that are previously unknown and accidentally discovered (e.g., treasure found in one's backyard). ***Zakat*** **Rate**: 20%.
>
> **Type II**: Known natural resources (e.g., agricultural land, mines, oil, and gas). ***Zakat*** **Rate**: 2.5%-10%, depending on certain factors.

Type III: Personal commercial wealth (e.g., gold, money, stocks, property). ***Zakat*** **Rate**: 2.5%.

The minimum amount of accumulated commercial resources that trigger *Zakat* is understood in various ways. In earlier times, *Zakat* was due on individuals who possessed 5 camels or 200 dirhams of pure silver. As most people no longer deal with gold or silver coins or keep livestock, modern standards are designed based upon the value of these assets, instead of their amount.

Since *Zakat* is a tax on wealth rather than income, it encourages reinvestment of wealth, as failing to do so may result in a 2.5% annual depreciation. This discourages hoarding and can stimulate the economy for everyone's benefit.

In Islamic teachings, while voluntary charitable donations are strongly encouraged and, in some cases are obligatory, they are not enforceable by any authority. These donations are a matter between an individual and Allah (SWT), the Provider of all resources. However, *Zakat* is considered an enforceable obligation and, as such, is akin to a tax. This was the understanding of the first generation of Muslims about this concept, some say, based upon the following *ayah*:

Al-Quran 9:103 "Take from their wealth 'O Prophet' charity to purify and bless them, and pray for them – surely your prayer is a source of comfort for them. And Allah is All-Hearing, All-Knowing".

During the life of Prophet Muhammad (SAW), people followed *Zakat* rules with minimal resistance. However, after his passing, some individuals and groups refused to fulfill this obligation, which led to a legal action against them by the newly established government. Following this precedent, later Muslim governments followed and established the government-based *Zakat* system.

In present times, government enforcement of *Zakat* rules creates confusion, anger and mistrust, even among religiously minded well-intentioned people. Unlike in the distant past, the issue now is less about people's unwillingness to pay. The mistrust or ill-will is mostly due to a double standard that government employs, in addition to a lack of full transparency and accountability. The double standard is due to a fundamental disagreement resulting from the concept of taxation on part of the government. Aided by the religious establishment, modern Muslim governments differentiate between what they collect as "taxes" versus what they impose as "*Zakat*". Taxes, for this discussion, is an amount a government may charge its citizens for whatever reason or justification, religious or non-religious, and can use its forces to collect if not voluntarily given. Practically, other than the rates and rules described above, there is no difference whatsoever: Both "taxes" and the "Zakat" are clearly taxation on part of government, except that one has a religious basis.

As far as its governance is concerned, individuals are free to calculate and deliver *Zakat* amount to their choice of recipients, which may include government agencies. Problem arises when some people with larger assets or a whole section of a society refuse to fulfill this religious injunction. Though it is not the state's role or responsibility to police people about their religious obligations, the *Zakat* has a different dimension. First, by definition, it is not just between an individual and Allah (SWT) (like the *salat* or fasting): Another person, the recipient of *Zakat* is involved. Every society needs resources to cater for the needs of orphans, poor, elderly, and disable. One solution might be to impose a universal across-the-board tax, but that would be unfair for people who already are needy. Islam's solution for this issue is the system of *Zakat* and without it, a large part of societal injustice and problems may remain unresolved.

Zakat can be given to relatives or even to a husband by his wife, if financially deserving (In Islam, husband and wife may have separate finances). In fact, giving Zakat to relatives is encouraged as its spiritual value is higher than giving it to an outside agency. In this regard, scholars have considered certain relatives (parents, children, and wife) to be excluded from this list of recipients, as meeting their basic financial needs is a primary obligation for the *Zakat* payer.

The obligation of *Zakat* can be dealt in privacy, or in private manner, but in the broader context, the recommended recipients of *Zakat* in a society are better served through a concerted government effort. This obligation entails availability of resources for the ruling authority, thus providing it a fiscal justification to acquire this amount. This is especially the case for its collection from people and entities with larger assets. This exactly what happened right after the Prophet (SAW) passed away. Governing authority of that time compelled people to pay by taking a legal action, thus cementing *Zakat*'s status as a government enforced taxation.

What if people have mass-scale distrust of their government, or if the government is declaratively, not Islamic, like the U.S.A? This concern is also valid regarding the present-day Muslim countries whose governing structures, financial systems, and the system of taxation may not follow Islamic rules and regulations.

Before delving into governance, let's dive deeper into the use of *Zakat* funds:

Al-Quran 9:60: "Alms-tax is only for the poor and the needy, for those employed to administer it, for those whose hearts are attracted to the faith, for freeing slaves, for those in debt, for Allah's cause, and for needy travelers. This is an obligation from Allah. And Allah is All-Knowing, All-Wise."

Many claim that *Zakat* funds can only benefit Muslims, though this idea is not supported by the Qur'an or the *Hadith*. The recipients of *Zakat* or the causes supported by it are equally important for any form of governance or its citizens, Muslim or non-Muslim. It would be unwise for a government to ask a poor about their religion before providing any assistance. It will also be unfair and discriminatory, as governments are responsible for all its citizens in a non-discriminatory manner. For example, U.S. Federal and State governments collect taxes to fund various services for its disabled, elderly, and poor citizens & residents, without discrimination. Almost 50% of every tax dollar is used to fund these causes. These are the same causes that would be prioritized by a *Zakat* department, if it was a Muslim government.

Some point to early Islamic history, where Muslims and non-Muslims had different social and legal arrangements. Non-Muslims under Muslim rule paid the *Jizya* tax, while Muslims paid *Zakat*; both were taxes based on ability to pay, exempting the poor, elderly, and disabled. Both are rooted in the Qur'an (2:177, 9:60). While *Jizya* was often justified as a substitute for military service or protection, these reasons are less relevant today with integrated militaries and constitutional rights. Now, the core rationale for such taxes is fairness, much like *Zakat*.

Now, let's consider the government's role in *Zakat* collection. It's not uncommon in Muslim-majority countries like Pakistan for people to question whether their government even represents Islamic values and thus their hesitancy to pay *Zakat* to one of its agencies. For people in the U.S.A., there is no such confusion, as its government is by design not Islamic. But does this even matter?

Additionally, there's the matter of taxes collected by the government in addition to *Zakat*. In early Muslim governments, *Zakat* was the only obligatory tax. Today, governments and, what I may call, the aiding religious scholars distinguish between *Zakat* and other forms of taxation. This distinction is arbitrary and unfair to citizens, as *Zakat* is the priority, and any tax collected by the government should first be counted towards that obligation. In practical terms, the religious establishment has a clear conflict of interest, as, in addition to the government's *Zakat* department, they maintain their own *Zakat* collection system. It is in their interest to make a distinction between the two.

The practice of deducting *Zakat* directly from salaries was common in early Muslim governments to fund public welfare. Now in present times, governments make arbitrary distinction and call the same amount a "tax" and demand a separate amount for the "*Zakat*". In addition, the same system charges a significant amount of General Sales Tax on almost everything, including utilities, which is gross injustice to the poor and needy, who are supposed to be helped by taxation.

For those of us living in non-Muslim societies, nearly 50% of the taxes we pay go toward supporting the poor, elderly, and disabled. Below are the figures for U.S. government spending:

Federal Government Spending:

- Social Security (Elderly, Disabled): 21-23%
- Medicare (Elderly, Disabled): 14-15%
- Medicaid and other health programs (Low income, Disabled): 12-16%
- Safety Net Programs (Food Assistance, Housing, Welfare, etc.): 8-10%
- **Total: 50-60% of Federal taxes.**

State Spending:

- Medicaid & Healthcare (Low income and disabled): 25-30%

- Public Assistance & Social Services: 5-10%
- **Total: 25-40% of State taxes.**

So, what should a person do? For those, who may align with above arguments, there might be an alternate strategy. First, a taxpayer may calculate the approximate portion of their taxes already supporting the *Zakat* eligible causes. Any government asking them to pay more taxes, by labeling it *Zakat*, must first acknowledge the amount already paid to that effect. Afterwards, the amount can be adjusted with additional amount if it was less than the alms-tax due from the taxpayer. Ignoring this fact leads to financial injustice, and in Islam, financial injustice in any form is unjustified, akin to taking a fight with Allah SWT, and Allah SWT knows the best.

Chapter 11

The *Ardh* and the *Samawaat*

The Physicals, non-physicals, and in-between

The principal subject matter of the Qur'an, directly or indirectly, is about Allah SWT, His Authority and His Dominion. It addresses this subject in a variety of ways, which can be further divided in two major parts: The first is about the matters of the *Ghaib*. The *Ghaib* is usually translated as Unseen, but this translation is misleading and does not convey its real meaning. An unborn child in mother's womb used to be unseen, or if rain is going to come in a few days or not, or what a person is doing right now living on the opposite side of the world are examples of matters that for us used to be unseen, but not anymore. Like that, we like to see or experience if there is life on Mars or any other planet. All such matters do not come under the category of the *Ghaib*. Some words of the Qur'an like the *Riba* and the *Ghaib* are better not translated in a single word or expression, as translation can be easily misleading. In the translated text, they should be used as such, and an explanation based upon the context can be separately provided.

The matters in the *Ghaib* category are those that are not accessible to most human beings to see or experience in this life, at least not unless Allah SWT makes an exception. We do not and cannot appropriately see or experience Allah SWT. The situation for us is same regarding angels, *jinns*, Afterlife, *Jannah* or *Jahannam*. These matters are the matter of *Ghaib* for us. As critical part of *Iman* or Faith, our understanding about these subjects, or the *Ghaib*, is a matter of belief. Knowing our limitations, the Qur'an repeatedly reminds us of and coaxes us, directly and indirectly, to have a strong belief.

The situation about many other matters in the Qur'an, which might be accessible to us to see, experience, or explore in this life, is different. This category includes everything that is not *Ghaib*. As the list of these matters can be so large that oceans may not be enough to write about them if they become ink:

Al-Qur'an 31:27 *"If all the trees on earth were pens and the ocean 'were ink', refilled by seven other oceans, the Words of Allah would not be exhausted. Surely Allah is Almighty, All-Wise."*

They are discussed in a broad sense with some exceptions. Main wording or the concepts used for this category are *ardh* and *samawaat*. The word *ardh* appears over 400 times, *samaa* over 300 times, and the pair *ardh* and *samawaat* together more than 200 times. Indeed, one or the other is mentioned on nearly every page of the Qur'an. Despite this ubiquity, to claim that the scholars have or had full grasp of the meaning of these words every place they appear in the Qur'an, is inaccurate.

As discussed in an earlier chapter, interpreting the Qur'an is a dynamic and multi-layered process. This is true with both subject matters: matters of the *Ghaib* and the rest, including what we call the natural or scientific. Though the *Ghaib* might be beyond our full comprehension, we have better chance understanding the natural subjects. They provide us indirect clues and evidence about the *Ghaib*. Learning about them, reflecting, exploring, and researching them is strongly promoted. This exercise may bring us closer to understanding our Creator, Allah SWT, the Creator of all imaginable and unimaginable entities and things. Additionally, as our knowledge of nature and science evolves, so does our understanding of certain Qur'anic *ayat*.

In this chapter, I have tried to reflect on the specific concepts of *ardh* and *samawaat*, as they appear in the Qur'an, with a hope that it may coax the reader to think and further research this subject. It is not my position, and not of any good teacher for that matter, to provide explicit answer to every question. It is better to talk about the ways to find the right answer. Unraveling divine instructions is an individual effort and a never-ending lifelong process.

To help us understand this subject better and especially to appreciate the diversity of meaning for these words, I created a list of subject matters, which these words convey while appearing in different parts of the Qur'an.

1. What may be obvious to a human being

In this context, the concept of *ardh* seems straightforward: the land known to human beings, or the planet Earth itself. For example:

Al-Quran 47:10 *"Have they not travelled throughout the land to see what was the end of those before them? Allah annihilated them, and a similar fate awaits the disbelievers."*

Here, the word *ardh*, translated as "land," appears to refer to different parts of the planet Earth—the only planet, in our current understanding, known to sustain intelligent life.

In some other verses, *ardh* and *samaa* are mentioned together in this manner:

Al-Quran 2:22 *"Who has made the earth a resting place for you, and the sky as a canopy, and sent down rain from the sky and brought forth therewith fruits as a provision for you. Then do not set up rivals unto Allah (in worship) while you know (that He Alone has the right to be worshipped)."*

Al-Quran 79:27–33 *"Which is harder to create: you or the sky? He built it, raising it high and forming it flawlessly. He dimmed its night and brought forth its daylight. As for the earth, He spread it out as well, bringing forth its water and pastures and setting the mountains firmly 'upon it'—all as 'a means of' sustenance for you and your animals."*

For human beings, *ardh* in 2:22 clearly refers to the planet Earth—their dwelling place. The term *samaa*, used here in the singular form, differs from its plural *samawaat* in other verses. In this case, it may signify the visible sky or the atmosphere surrounding the Earth. Some translators render it as "heavens." The Qur'an describes it as a canopy over the Earth, a metaphor that resonates with modern scientific understanding. A more precise rendering might be "aerosphere," the body of air enveloping our planet.

This atmosphere sustains life and shields it, enabling winds, rain, and other weather phenomena, while also protecting the Earth from harmful solar radiation, including ultraviolet and gamma rays. Without it, life on Earth would not be possible.

The term *samaa*—whether in singular form or plural (*samawaat*)—carries different meanings in other contexts. It may not be obvious for a cursory reader of the Qur'an in Arabic or its translation. It has been translated in a variety of ways by different scholars—sometimes as "heaven," "sky," "firmament," "universe," or "space" (e.g., 79:27–33 and 41:9–12). To avoid making this discussion overly technical, I have not cited every reference here, as they can be easily explored. What matters is the range of interpretations. The following example from 51:47 shows how translators render *samaa* differently:

Al-Quran 51:47 "We built the universe with 'great' might, and We are certainly expanding 'it'." *(Mustafa Khattab)*

"With the power and skill did We construct the Firmament: for it is We Who create the vastness of Space." *(Abdullah Yusuf Ali)*

"And the sky was built by Us with might; and indeed We are the expanders." *(Taqi Usmani)*

"With power did We construct the heaven. Verily, We are Able to extend the vastness of space thereof." *(Al-Hilali and Khan)*

Clearly, in English—and in scientific terms—words like *universe, firmament, sky,* or *heaven* may not mean the same thing. Thus, our understanding of an *ayah's* message may shift depending on which rendering we accept. And the difference in translation is not just due to the linguistic differences. It reflects translators' understanding of the word *samaa* in this ayah. A reader may easily understand this by reflecting on the differences between the concepts of "sky" and "universe". Is the *ayah* talking about the sky being expanded or the universe? which are two different things. I hope you get my point.

2. Dichotomy of *Ardh* and *Samawaat*

Like many other concepts in the Qur'an, *ardh* and *samawat* are frequently mentioned together, almost as a duality—contrasting yet interconnected, like day and night, man and woman, and other paired ideas. When used in this way, the terms convey meanings that differ from the more direct usage described earlier.

If *samaa* in singular form already carries multiple possible meanings, translators face even greater difficulty with its plural form, *samawaat.* Common translations include "heavens," "firmaments," or "skies." For example, in the following single verse, Abdullah Yusuf Ali translates it in two different ways:

Al-Quran 2:29"*It is He Who hath created for you all things that are on earth; then He turned to heaven and made them into seven firmaments; and of all things He hath perfect knowledge.*"

Yet, in another verse, he renders *samawaat* differently:

Al-Quran 71:15"*See you not how Allah has created the seven heavens one above another.*"

For clarification, following is translation of these words in Merrium-Webster dictionary:

Heaven(s): The expanse of space that seems to be over the earth like a dome.

Firmament: The vault or arch of the sky.

Despite the range of translations available, questions remain about whether these renderings truly capture the essence of the original text. A cursory reader may not scrutinize these subtleties. Even if it is done, including consulting classical exegesis, one may find a diversity of interpretations—none of which offer definitive clarity. With the proliferation of AI tools, it is now easier for readers to explore these varied perspectives, yet the fundamental uncertainty persists. This ongoing ambiguity serves as a reminder that our understanding of such concepts remains, for now, beyond our complete comprehension.

Now let's look at a different subject: A closer look at the translation of the first part of Al-Quran 2:29:

Al-Quran 2:29 *"It is He Who hath created for you all things that are on earth; then He turned to heaven and made them into seven firmaments; and of all things He hath perfect knowledge."*

Paying close attention, a reader may notice significant variations in translation of the underlined part of the *ayah*. For example, it is, "on earth," by Abdullah Yusuf Ali, and "in the earth" by Marmaduke Pickthall, Ahmad Zaki Hammad, and Dr. Mustafa Khattab. While Muhammad Taqi Usmani worded it differently, "all that the earth contains". In may also be, "within or among earth." Does accepting one translation over the other make any difference? It absolutely does, if only one reflects little deeper. Depending upon the choice, this subtlety narrows or broadens the concept of *ardh*.

Let me try to explain the differences: Things "on earth" include what lies on the surface – e.g., mountains, oceans, humans, animals, plants; things "in the earth" may also include things that are inside the earth – e.g., water, oil, minerals; and the concept of "within or among earth" include all of the above and the earth itself – in a way, all physical mater wherever or whatever form it is. Finally, *ardh* is contrasted with *samawaat*, which must be different but somehow also paired with it.

The Qur'an describes *samawaat* as consisting of seven layers or "firmaments." But what are these? Are these the seven skies around planets like Earth, Mars, or the Moon? That seems unlikely, as there are too many planets like them. Are these seven universes? Possible, though evidence so far is lacking. Is this about the seven dimensions? May be. Some physicists propose multiple dimensions—seven or more—as in the string theory. Still, this remains speculative. Can this be something altogether beyond human comprehension? Perhaps, though its frequent mention in the Qur'an suggests it is not entirely inaccessible to us. It is not a matter of the *Ghaib.* It may just be pointing to something real and present everywhere, just beneath our intellectual radar.

One striking parallel is the seven layers of the electromagnetic spectrum recognized in modern science:

1. **Radio Waves** — longest wavelength, lowest frequency; used for broadcasting, radar, GPS, Wi-Fi.

2. **Microwaves** — used in cooking, satellite communication, radar.

3. **Infrared (IR)** — thermal imaging, night vision, remote controls.

4. **Visible Light** — enabling human vision and illumination.

5. **Ultraviolet (UV)** — sterilization, tanning, counterfeit detection.

6. **X-Rays** — medical imaging, cancer treatment, security.

7. **Gamma Rays** — highest energy; used in medicine and astrophysics.

It is possible that what we recognize as electromagnetic waves corresponds to just one layer, while others remain unknown. Could the strong and weak nuclear forces also be part of this reality? Perhaps—a reflection that hints at a unified framework of origin or creation.

In *Hadith* literature, *samawaat* is vividly described in the account of the Prophet Muhammad's (SAW) Night Journey (*Miraj*). Scholars have long debated whether this journey was physical or spiritual. If we accept Allah's omnipotence, either is possible. In the famous narration, the Prophet (SAW) traveled through seven "heavens", meeting angels and prophets—from Adam (AS) to Ibrahim (AS). These heavens seemed physical, yet the beings encountered were beyond ordinary human perception, suggesting dimensions both physical and metaphysical. These meetings suggest that the heavens are not merely physical domains but also encompass realities that transcend human perception. While the journey features elements that appear physical, the presence of metaphysical beings and realms points to an interplay between the material and the immaterial. This duality aligns with broader Qur'anic themes, where descriptions of creation frequently blend the physical with the spiritual, inviting reflection on realities beyond everyday experience.

The Qur'an was revealed as guidance for our lived reality, but it also points to dimensions beyond it. While its subject matter addresses the physical world, it simultaneously reflects the spiritual—often through metaphor and layered meaning. Its archetypal concepts, like *ardh* and *samawaat*, may also carry both physical and spiritual dimensions. Ultimately, Allah (SWT) knows best.

Humans have long been reflecting on the idea of origin of life, and in addition, on the origin of everything around them, living or non-living and physical or non-physical.

Ancient philosophers in different parts of the world, including from China and India to Egypt and Greece, speculated and provided multitudes of opinions. In recent times, influenced by somewhat deeper understanding of Physics and Mathematics, contemporary theoretical physicists provide their own explanation, e.g., the so-called string theory. The Quran also provides clues about this question:

Al-Quran 21:30 *"Do the disbelievers not realize that the heavens and earth were 'once' one mass then We split them apart? And We created from water every living thing. Will they not then believe?"*

Al-Quran 35:1 *"Praise be to Allah, Who created (out of nothing) the heavens and the earth, …"*

Ayah 21:30 implies a primordial or an initial state of everything, before it was divided into the *samawaat* and *ardh*, all non-physical and the physical things. With that understanding, one may also wonder, where did the primordial state come from? Whatever answer one may come up for that question, the same question will arise again; until we reach a point where we must accept that, logically speaking, things have come out of nothing (to our understanding). Part of this can be understood in a different way: Material is made up of molecules and molecules are made up of atoms. Atoms are made of electrons, neutrons and protons, and these are made up of sub-atomic particles. The sub-atomic particles are made of smaller sub-atomic particles, until we reach a point where no material (or *ardh*) may exist as any material like it can logically be further split. Anything beyond must exist in another or transitional state, possibly resembling a wave or waves of energy (the *samawaat*). In scientific terms, at that level, *ardh* and *samawaat* become interchangeable.

This concept is taken even further with the *ayah* 35:1, where the key word is *Fathir*, again difficult to translate in English. Its root word is "*fitr* – *fa*, *thaw*, and *ra*," whose meaning included, to create, bring into being, but also to split or cleave. The derivative of this word used in the *ayah* is *Fathir*, which encompasses both meanings. Allah SWT not only is the Creator, but He is also the One who split them into *ardh* and *samawaat*, the physical matter and non-physicals.

The word *Fathir* also appears in the *ayah* 42:11and translated as the Originator of *samawaat* and *ardh*. In addition, like their paired nature, some other pairing is mentioned, including the ability to hear and see, all clues for us to reflect on.

Al Quran 42:11 *"'He is' the Originator of the heavens and* *the earth. He has made for you spouses from among yourselves, and 'made' mates for cattle 'as well'—multiplying you 'both'. There is nothing like Him, for He 'alone' is the All-Hearing, All-Seeing."*

Some more detail about the concept of *samawaat* is given in the following verse, usually translated as heavens:

Al-Quran 13:2 *"It is Allah Who has raised the heavens without pillars—as you can see—then established Himself on the Throne. He has subjected the sun and the moon, each orbiting for an appointed term. He conducts the whole affair. He makes the signs clear so that you may be certain of the meeting with your Lord."*

The word "*aamad*" is translated as "pillars" following the translation of the word "*rafaa*" as "raised (something physically raised)." These words are metaphorical and can also be translated as "support" instead of pillars and "elevate" (physically or spiritually). Even if taken in physical terms, this verse can be compared with another verse, 78:7, where the support system of *ardh* with mountain is emphasized. Solid structures are strengthened by support of solid structures. On the other hand, if we understand *samawaat* as non-physical matter, which may not require that kind of support, the message becomes clear. Some might say that pillars here is about the apparent lack of physical support system for planets and galaxies. But that would not make sense as they do have underlying support keeping them in the manner they are, which to our present understanding is due to interplay of their inertia and gravitational pull to each other. The tantalizing question about that is that at the end, this system is an interplay of both physical and non-physical entities and at deeper levels they merge into one another.

Here is another way to differentiate between *ardh* and *samaawat*:

Al-Quran 39:67 *"They have not shown Allah His proper reverence—when on the Day of Judgment, the 'whole' earth will be in His Grip, and the heavens will be rolled up in His Right Hand. Glorified and Exalted is He above what they associate 'with Him'!"*

First, it is an important reminder, that many words and concepts in the Qur'an are metaphorical, like the Hand of Allah SWT. Instead of "the 'whole' earth" and "the heavens," the verse makes more sense and significance if these words are taken as "all physical," and "the non-physical" matter. The choice of the words "*qabaza*," indicating control of all *ardh* or all physical matter, and "*matiwiyyat*," indicating the capturing or rolling up of non-physical things, which, as we know, exist like waves, help us understand their differences.

4. Something in between *ardh* and *samawaat*

In some *ayat*, another concept is introduced, "*bayyana-huma*" *ardh* and *samawaat*: something in between these two concepts:

Al-Quran 15:85 "*We have not created the heavens and the earth and everything in between except for a purpose. And the Hour is certain to come, so forgive graciously.*"

Al-Quran 43:85 "*And Blessed is the One to Whom belongs the kingdom of the heavens and the earth and everything in between! With Him 'alone' is the knowledge of the Hour. And to Him you will 'all' be returned.*"

Al-Quran 44:38-39 "*We did not create the heavens and the earth and everything in between for sport. We only created them for a purpose, but most of these 'pagans' do not know.*"

After emphasizing that everything is created for a purpose, we are introduced to a new concept of something "in-between" *ardh* and *samawaat*. What we understand by this concept may differ based upon what we may understand by the terms *ardh* and *samawaat*. If we take *ardh* as the planet Earth and *samawaat* as skies, we have difficulty figuring out the meaning of the in-between. Does it imply all the planets we could see from Earth, or exist? Possible, but it is not clear. Let's say if someone is talking about something, "in-between" Massachusetts and California, do they mean every place between these two states, or rather an undefined place, which is neither in Mass nor in California, somewhere in-between? It is not clear. In addition, in this example, the extent or the boundaries, from coast to coast, are clearly defined. But that is not the case with *ardh* and *samawaat*, for which, based upon conventional understanding, the nature and extent of boundaries are not clearly defined. Many translators have used "between", instead of "in-between" to translate "*bayyana-huma*." I consider it contextualization instead of linguistic accuracy, based upon their version of understanding of *ardh* and *samawaat*. Finally, if the purpose of mentioning the concept of "in-between" was to talk about totality or everything, it does not seem to be the case as, in a different verse, that concept is explicitly mentioned in a different way:

Al-Quran 2:255 *"Allah! There is no god ⌜worthy of worship⌝ except Him, the Ever-Living, All-Sustaining. Neither drowsiness nor sleep overtakes Him. To Him belongs <u>whatever is in the heavens and whatever is on the earth</u>. Who could possibly intercede with Him without His permission? He ⌜fully⌝ knows what is ahead of them and what is behind them, but no one can grasp any of His knowledge—except what He wills ⌜to reveal⌝. His Seat encompasses* *the heavens and the earth, and the preservation of both does not tire Him. For He is the Most High, the Greatest."*

Reference to the concept of "in-between" *ardh* and *samawaat* is different from "whatever" is in the heavens and "whatever" is on the earth, and not without a purpose. It gets more interesting, if, in the verse 2:255, instead of usual understanding we interpret "*ardh*" as all physical, and "*samawaat*" as all non-physical matter (as discussed in the next part). With that understanding, there are things or concepts that are difficult to fit in either of these categories. One common and may be easier to understand such concept is a shadow of anything, which does not fit in either of these concepts, but we do perceive it. In addition, in the world observable to a human being, concepts of magnetism, gravity, and above all, time are difficult to fit in either category. Both magnetism and gravity are sometimes stated as physical phenomenon, but they don't have any physicality. Similarly, their quality as a wave is not definable as a typical wave form either. It is like they are neither this nor that, something in-between. Even sound has some similarities to a shadow but discussing that might be too technical for this writing. Concept of time of course is an entirely different and may be easier to understand as it is neither physical nor a wave like concept. Can these be examples of the "in-between" concepts?

In the spiritual realms for a human perception, examples of things in-between *ardh* and *samawaat*, might be the angels and *jinns*. Only Allah SWT knows best. The layered understanding of *samawaat* offers a profound perspective, blending spiritual and physical interpretations with scientific parallels. From a scientific standpoint, waves and matter are never fully separate; they merge and transform into one another, suggesting a shared, unified origin.

5. The Originator of Everything

The topic of how anything or everything originated is somewhat different than who might have started it. I reflected on the former part above and the following account is about the latter. Reflecting on this question brings us to the topic of Allah (SWT): Does He exist? If we say yes, what argument we might have for His existence? From the ancient philosophers' discourses to the YouTube presentations of our times, human beings continue to reflect and argue about this subject. Muslim scholars had their own share of arguments, and probably the most famous or quoted ones were from Ibn Sina and some of its critique by Al-Ghazali, which I will try to briefly outline at the end of this section.

For a reader who may not be interested in deeper reflection of this subject, the argument may be straight-forward: It is so, because that's what is written in the Qur'an, or the *Hadith*. This understanding works well for them but may not convince a non-believer. It may not satisfy a reflective believer either. May be that was the reason that scholars like Ibn Sina and Al-Ghazali made their arguments. Before I provide an outline of what these arguments might have been, let's review what the Qur'an says about this topic.

I used the terms, "anything or everything" above, which may seem different from *ardh* and *samawaat*, but for the question we are trying to answer, it does not make much difference. We are trying to find who is the originator or creator of anything or everything, including *ardh* and *samawaat.*

There are numerous references in the Qur'an mentioning Allah (SWT) being the Creator or Originator of everything in multiple different ways. Let's look at a few *ayat* with this subject:

Al-Quran 2:117 *"He is the Originator of the heavens and the earth! When He decrees a matter, He simply tells it, "Be!" And it is!"*

Al-Quran 6:101–102 *"He is the Originator of the heavens and the earth. How could He have children when He has no mate? He created all things, and He has perfect knowledge of everything. That is Allah—your Lord! There is no god worthy of worship except Him. He is the Creator of all things, so worship Him alone. And He is the Maintainer of everything."*

Al-Quran 29:20 *"Say, O Prophet, 'Travel throughout the land and see how He originated the creation, then Allah will bring it into being one more time. Surely Allah is Most Capable of everything.'"*

In the above passages, *samawaat* and *ardh*—translated as "heavens and earth"—refer to the totality of created existence, encompassing both the physical and non-physical realms. This broader sense is reinforced in another verse:

Al-Quran 7:54 *"Indeed, your Lord is Allah, Who created the heavens and the earth in six Days, then established Himself on the Throne. He makes the day and night overlap in rapid succession. He created the sun, the moon, and the stars—all subjected to His command. The creation and the command belong to Him alone. Blessed is Allah—Lord of all worlds!"*

Here, "heavens and earth" imply the entirety of creation. Limiting their scope to merely the skies and the planet Earth diminish the richness of intended meaning. The Qur'an consistently distributes knowledge of such profound realities across multiple passages.

Allah's role as the Originator of *samawaat* and *ardh* is affirmed throughout the Qur'an (e.g., 6:14, 6:79, 6:101). His act of creation is repeatedly emphasized (e.g., 2:284, 3:109, 3:129, 4:126, 4:131–132, 4:170–171). Furthermore, the underlying truth or principle behind creation is highlighted in 6:73, while His absolute dominion over creation is described in many places (e.g., 2:107, 5:17–18, 5:40, 5:120).

Perhaps most famously, the *Ayat al-Kursi* (2:255) encapsulates His sovereignty:

Al-Quran 2:255 *"Allah! There is no god worthy of worship except Him, the Ever-Living, the All-Sustaining. Neither drowsiness nor sleep overtakes Him. To Him belongs whatever is in the heavens and whatever is on the earth. Who can intercede with Him except by His permission? He fully knows what is ahead of them and what is behind them, and they cannot grasp any of His knowledge except what He wills. His Throne encompasses the heavens and the earth, and preserving them does not tire Him. For He is the Most High, the Greatest."*

Here, the expression *"whatever is in the heavens and whatever is on the earth"* may also be understood as *"whatever is or within the heavens, and whatever is or within the earth."* This broader reading prevents any limitation of scope, underscoring Allah's dominion over everything created, both physical and non-physical. Similarly, the phrase *"His Throne encompasses the heavens and the earth"* signifies His authority and sustaining power over all realms—both within and beyond human understanding, present or future.

For a believer, the Quran is the highest authority and reading the above *ayat* should not leave any doubt about the ultimate Originator of everything, including *ardh* and *samawaat*. But this matter is not that simple or straightforward. May be that is the reason that this subject is reiterated numerous times in the Qur'an, frequently in a coaxing manner to reflect on this subject. And as I stated above, a non-believer or a person of reflection might have to dive deeper to fully fathom and accept this truth. If the reader does not have any issues with this subject, the next part in smaller fonts can be skipped. On the other hand, for anyone interested in a little deeper intellectual dive, which I hope most would try, take a deep breath and enjoy:

> In this section, I briefly talk about the arguments of Ibn Sina and Al-Ghazali, may Allah (SWT) have mercy on both. I am mentioning this account here with a hope that more people or Muslims may pay attention to it, which it deserves. One may also read it online or listen to a lecture on YouTube about this subject. Some have said that with this logical analysis, Ibn Sina has made the best philosophical argument for existence of Allah (SWT). His argument works like this:
>
> A. Allah (SWT), by definition, is One and there is no other entity like Him. He is the Creator and the Sustainer of every other thing. He is neither created by any other

entity nor is He dependent upon any. He is the Omnipotent, the Omnipresent and the Permanent, and He is not bound by such concepts as space and time.

B. Logically speaking, imagine every possible thing or entity, including Allah (SWT), that may exist. We may divide them in two types, things that are contingent, and things that are non-contingent.

C. Contingent things are those that may or may not exist, and if they exist, they exist from a cause or dependency. According to Ibn Sina, contingent things fall under '*mumkin al-wajood*' or possible existent. They may exist if conditions were right or they were "caused" to exist, or they may not exist. This includes every physical and non-physical thing, living and non-living, including *ardh* and *samawaat*, wherever and whenever it exists.

D. Non-contingent is something that must exist, cannot not exist, have always existed, and does not have a cause or dependency for existence. Ibn Sina called it '*al-wajib al-*

wajood,' or the *necessary* existent, which, in a sense, is the description of Allah (SWT).

E. For clarification, it is important to understand the meaning of the cause in this context, as explained by Ibn Sina. If you look at a house, it is not existing just because someone built it, which is also true and one of its contingencies; rather the house is existing because of complex arrangements of bricks and other materials, and the intrinsic nature of all that material. The builder only put the house together, which came into being because of the above causes and could not have existed without them.

F. Clarifying it further, in the list of contingent things are all imaginable physical and non-physical things, including *ardh* and *samawaat*, living or non-living, e.g., the building of a house or the electricity turning our lights on. They only exist because of something else, or a cause. For example, I exist because of complex arrangements of cells in my body and a specific environment with certain amount of oxygen. Every cell of my body exists because of a similarly complex arrangement of biomolecules. These molecules exist because of an arrangement of atoms; they exist because of an arrangement of subatomic particles, and they exist because of a complex arrangement of whatever they are made up of. This series can keep going as every possible thing or entity we might discover or think about, would have some basic mechanism or cause to exist upon which it depends upon or is contingent upon.

G. None of the contingent entities can qualify as the necessary existent, or '*al-wajib al-wajood*', as they all, alone or as a group, are themselves caused by or dependent upon something else. For example, no human being can have such claim as they can easily collapse if there was a mild alteration of underlying cellular arrangement. Even the healthiest person in the world ultimately cease to exist. Same argument can be applied to anything in this category, physical or non-physical.

H. Since we and the universe exists, there must be a cause for this existence. The cause of all possible existents can be within the same category of possible existent '*mumkin al-wajood* 'or out of it.

I. If we say that the cause of everything that exists is within the category of possible existents, it cannot be the necessary existent, as everything in this category is contingent. Even if we say that the things together in this category, in a smaller group or altogether, is that cause, it does not work because of the same problem.

J. Logically speaking, as explained above, this cause or contingency cannot be something that itself requires a cause or contingency. It must be an entity out of this category of possible existents. This entity must have always existed and would always exist, as any such limitation, including time, creates a type of contingency.

K. In this category of the necessary existent, there cannot be more than one entity as having more than one will create a necessity of differentiating between the two, which is a contingency, and is not allowed. This is what Ibn Sina called '*al-wajib al-wajood*,' translated as the necessary existent.

L. The necessary existent must not have any physical parts, as that also creates a contingency.

M. The necessary existent must not be bound by concepts of space and time, which are also contingencies.

N. Finally, the only logical conclusion is that the cause or contingency of everything, including *ardh* and *samawaat*, must be outside of the category of *mumkin al-wajood*, the possible existent category. Any entity, force, or any other such concept belonging to this category has a contingency, cause, or dependency and cannot belong to the category of the necessary existent or the *al-wajib al-wajood*.

O. As we and everything around us exists, the responsible cause or the necessary existent must also exist.

P. As stated at the top, and as per Qur'anic definition, Allah (SWT) fits in the category

> of the Necessary Existent. With this exercise, Ibn Sina was able to provide justification and logical proof of the existence of Allah (SWT), an entity different from and the cause of everything else.

As far as the difference of opinion between Ibn Sina and Al-Ghazali, books have been written about this subject, and I am not going to go into any such detail. For our context here, Al-Ghazali, without rejecting it altogether, undermined the value of rational or logical way of reflection & gaining knowledge, especially the knowledge of concepts considered deep for human understandings, the topmost being the knowledge about Allah (SWT). According to his understanding, the practice of human reasoning and logical or philosophical analysis has a lower ceiling and the higher level of knowledge is achieved by intuition or revelation by the Divine intervention. In his critique of the works of ancient and some Muslim philosophers, like Ibn Sina, he provided examples where rational or philosophical thinking can be misleading and tantamount to unbelief. Though he was using philosophy itself to make his points, and by no means rejecting it altogether, majority of Muslim religious intellectuals or academia understood his message in that manner. This, to this day, has resulted in discarding or undermining the rational or philosophical thinking with a broad brush in the larger section of Muslim intellectual discourse, in a way, promotion of conformism. Some later philosophers, especially Ibn Rushd of Andalusia, critiqued al-Ghazali's work and tried to redirect this intellectual onslaught but in vain.

As I stated above, Muslim believers have different ways to accept the existence of Allah (SWT). For many, it is something they learned in their childhood and accept it as it is. For some others, if they pay attention to it, it is what is written in the Qur'an. For those, who dived deeper, the Qur'an mentions numerous indirect means of reflecting on this subject, including paying attention and reflecting on our own bodies and the universe around us. It coaxes us to review all that in a logical manner and learn from it. In a way, that's what Ibn Sina did. This is not to say that humans don't get more curious or like to have even deeper conviction. Prophet Musa may Allah (SWT) be please with him, despite the intuitive and divine knowledge granted to him, asked for a personal meeting.

6. The Underlying Principle

The Qur'an also addresses the issue of the underlying cause or the principle behind every created thing (as per human understanding):

Al-Quran 15:85 *"We have not created the heavens and the earth and everything in between except for a purpose. And the Hour is certain to come, so forgive graciously."*

Translating this ayah, scholars struggled with the word, "*haqq*", and interpreted it in multiple ways: "for a purpose" by Dr. Mustafa Khattab, "for just ends" by Abdullah Yusuf Ali, "for a true purpose" by Al-Hilali and Khan, "for a truthful purpose" by Muhammad Taqi Usmani, and "with truth" by Mahmood Khan. In this instance, the translation by Mahmood Khan, "We have not created heavens and the earth and everything in between except with truth" makes most linguistic sense. This *ayah* is alluding to the truth or the physical principles, the cause, or the physics, behind these creations.

To explain this issue further, let me digress a little. Mathematics is considered one of the fundamental subjects of human knowledge. For many, it is *the* fundamental subject, while some have called it the "divine" language, or the language of nature, upon which are based principles of all natural processes. To understand this issue, let's analyze a basic mathematical statement: $2 + 2 = 4$. Is this something we humans just made up, and then accepted it as truth? Or rather we discovered this notion with some reflection and experimentation? Not surprisingly, there are people on both sides of this argument: Some take the first position that mathematics is a made-up subject by humans, but most disagree. Their understanding is that humans are merely discovering the underlying truth. If we agree with the latter group, we can claim that we, humans, discovered an underlying truth or rule of nature, when we say $2 + 2 = 4$.

When Allah SWT states in the above *ayah* that *ardh* and *samawaat*, and everything in-between, implying everything created by Allah (SWT) is created with truth, that truth is the underlying principles or rules. We may call these rules or the principles mathematics or physics for our human understanding. We are not making up this stuff, either the mathematics or the physics, we just keep on reflecting and discovering its scope and depth.

After discussing the truth or the principles behind everything created, we must also talk about the intelligence behind. Let's say if we discover some light, which if falls upon an object help us see or define it. Principles of math and physics are that light, which expands our understanding of the world around us. In that analogy, we also like to know where the light is coming from, its source, and especially who put it there or made it possible so that we could find and use it. We may call that underlying intelligence, in comparison to the concept of underlying truth.

The Qur'an addresses this subject of the underlying intelligence behind all creation. It is described as *Noor* (usually translated as Light) in the following celebrated verse. While this verse warrants a separate and extensive discussion, it is important to note the deeply metaphorical and intellectually challenging nature of its imagery:

Al-Quran 24:35 *"Allah is the Light of the heavens and the earth. His light is like a niche containing a lamp; the lamp is enclosed in crystal, the crystal shining like a star, lit from a blessed olive tree, neither of the east nor of the west, whose oil would almost glow, even without fire touching it. Light upon light! Allah guides to His light whom He wills. And Allah presents parables to humanity. For Allah has perfect knowledge of all things."*

The Noor or the intelligence behind the truth (or the physics) of *ardh* and *samawaat,* is Allah SWT. Like many of His attributes, a little of that Noor is reflected upon human beings in different proportions, to some less and to others more. This Noor or His Intelligence is not completely hidden, rather it is always visible or accessible to anyone and everyone. Unlike any murky intelligence, His Noor is pure, like a crystal for human understanding. What humans have been asked to do in their lives has a singular purpose, to bring us closer to the source of this Noor.

7. HIS Dominion and Rule

These verses emphasize the absolute scope of Allah SWT's dominion, authority, and control over all of creation:

Al-Quran 3:83 *"Do they desire a way other than Allah's—when everything in the heavens and the earth submits to His will, willingly or unwillingly, and to Him they will all be returned?"*

Al-Quran 10:66 *"Surely, to Allah alone belongs all that is in the heavens and all that is on the earth. And what do those who associate others with Him truly follow? They follow nothing but assumptions and falsehood."*

Al-Quran 13:15 *"To Allah alone bow down in submission all that are in the heavens and the earth—willingly or unwillingly—as do their shadows, morning and evening."*

In these passages, the Arabic word "*mann*" has often been translated as "*all those*" or "*creatures.*" Linguistically, however, this is a contextualized rendering that may narrow the intended scope. A more precise translation could be "*whoever or whatever.*" This distinction is important: it highlights that Allah SWT is referring not only to sentient beings but to *all that exists*—everything within the *ardh* and *samawaat*, the physical and the non-physical realms—submitting to His will.

Verses such as 3:83 and 13:15 also point toward the metaphorical depth of the Qur'anic message. Submission (*sujood*) and bowing down are concepts that extend beyond human ritual; they apply, in a broader metaphysical sense, to every aspect of the universe. Matter, energy, natural laws, and unseen realities all "submit" by operating within the framework of His command. This invites deeper reflection on the metaphorical and cosmic dimensions of worship and obedience.

The Qur'an further affirms that Allah SWT encompasses, sustains, and has perfect knowledge of all that exists in the *samawaat* and the *ardh*—both physical and non-physical realms—as noted in verses such as 4:126, 6:3, and 10:61.

8. The Make-up of the Human Being

Beyond its cosmic meaning, the Qur'an also uses the concepts of *ardh* and *samawaat* to describe the human being and the origins of life itself. These terms not only represent the physical and non-physical realms on a universal scale but also apply to the very constitution of human existence. In this layer of understanding, *ardh* refers to the material substance—the elements, atoms, and molecules—that form the human body and sustain all living beings. By drawing attention to this connection, the Qur'an reminds humanity of its humble origins, grounding spiritual reflection in physical reality.

For example, the Qur'an recounts the message of Prophet

Salih (peace be upon him) to his people:

Al-Quran 11:61 *"And to the people of Thamud We sent their brother Ṣaliḥ. He said, 'O my people! Worship Allah. You have no god other than Him. He is the One Who produced you from the earth and settled you upon it. So seek His forgiveness and turn to Him in repentance. Surely my Lord is Ever Near, All-Responsive to prayers.'"*

Here, human beings are explicitly described as being produced from the *ardh.* This indicates not only their physical emergence from earthly materials but also their continued dependence upon it for survival.

This theme is further supported in other verses:

Al-Quran 71:17 *"And Allah has produced you from the earth, growing gradually."*

Al-Quran 40:67 *"He is the One Who created you from dust, then from a sperm-drop, then developed you into a clinging clot of blood, then He brings you forth as infants, so that you may reach your prime, and become old—though some of you may die sooner—reaching an appointed time, so perhaps you may understand Allah's power."*

In these verses, the translated word *dust* is interchangeable with *soil,* pointing again to the material basis of life. Modern science echoes this description: The human body is indeed composed of elements found in the earth—carbon, oxygen, hydrogen, nitrogen, calcium, and trace minerals—all of which originate in the physical matter of the natural world.

The Qur'an also draws attention to the *ardh* as a source of sustenance and renewal, as in the following verse:

Al-Quran 36:33 *"There is a sign for them in the dead earth: We give it life, producing grain from it for them to eat."*

By linking human origin with the soil and highlighting the continuous cycle of life emerging from the earth, these passages establish a deep connection between the human being and the natural world. The body is shaped by *ardh* and nourished by it, yet the soul belongs to a higher, non-physical dimension, reminding us of the dual nature of existence—earthly and divine, material and spiritual.

Related to this concept, the recommendation in Islam for burial of the human body after death differs from some other traditions. No chemicals are used or required, other than a simple washing with water, in many cases even not that, and there is no requirement for a coffin or a container. The body may be wrapped in a biodegradable cotton sheet and placed deep in the earth, or in some cases thrown in the seas, where it disintegrates into its basic elements from which it was originally created. This contrasts with practices like using toxic chemicals, wood or other materials to make a coffin, or burning the body:

all of which may pollute the natural environment and contribute to a positive carbon footprint, an injustice to the environment.

Al-Qur'an 20:55 *"From the (earth) did We create you, and into it shall We return you, and from it shall We bring you out once again."*

9. The Human Situation

From the beginning of human history, people have sought to understand their place in the universe and their relationship to the Creator. The Qur'an repeatedly invites us to reflect on the signs of Allah SWT in both the heavens (*samawaat*) and the earth (*ardh*), reminding us that nothing in creation exists without purpose. Some verses describe natural phenomena in language that appears simple on the surface yet carries unfolding layers of meaning as human knowledge progresses. What may once have been interpreted in purely literal terms can now be reconsidered considering scientific discovery, without diminishing the spiritual depth of the text. The verses discussed here open a window into this dialogue between revelation and human reflection, pointing us toward the underlying order of creation and the total submission of all things to their Creator.

Al-Quran 45:13 *"He [also] subjected for you whatever is in the heavens and whatever is on the earth—all by His grace. Surely in this are signs for people who reflect."*

Human beings, endowed with intellect, have been given countless ways to control, benefit from, and reflect upon the physical, the non-physical, and even the realities that lie in between.

Two other verses seem to provide even deeper and fascinating details:

Al-Quran 16:48–49 *"Have they not considered how the shadows of everything Allah has created incline to the right and the left [as the sun moves], totally submitting to Allah in all humility? And to Allah [alone] bows down [in submission] whatever is in the heavens and whatever is on the earth of living creatures, as do the angels—who are not too proud [to do so]."*

Traditionally, these verses are interpreted in the literal sense of shadows produced by sunlight. However, with our present understanding of creation, such an explanation becomes limited. For instance, how do we apply this to places where sunlight never reaches—such as deep caves on Earth, or the far side of the moon that remains hidden from the sun? In such environments, the usual concept of "shadow" does not exist. Likewise, in planetary systems with more than one sun, a single object may cast multiple shadows in different directions.

It seems more fitting to understand these words metaphorically. The phrase "to the right and the left" need not mean literal right and left, but rather "opposing directions." Similarly, the act of prostration (*sajdah*) for inanimate objects or animals is not physical bowing, but rather the fulfillment of their divinely assigned roles and attributes. Their submission lies in conforming perfectly to the laws of their nature (what Ibn Sina described as the cause), established by the Creator. And Allah (SWT) knows best.

Also, a shadow itself is not an independent entity—it has no substance or body of its own. It exists only as a phenomenon created when light is interrupted by a physical object. Attached to its base, its form depends entirely on the position of the light source. In that sense, a shadow is inseparable from the object it reflects, yet it has no independent qualities. Its very existence is a manifestation of the physical laws established by Allah SWT—its "*sajdah*" or submission to Him. Reflecting even deeper, these verses may be alluding to a fundamental physical principle underlying creation— e.g., what physicists describe as the "spin" of elementary particles, or perhaps some as-yet-unknown universal phenomenon.

Some other verses challenge our thinking even further, beyond the limits of our current understanding. For example:

Al-Quran 37:5–6 *"He is the Lord of the heavens and the earth and everything in between, and the Lord of all points of sunrise. Indeed,*

We have adorned the lowest heaven with the stars for decoration."

Here the key word is *mashaariq*, the plural of *mashriq*, usually translated as "the East"—the direction of sunrise. Conventionally, its plural is taken to mean different locations of sunrise at different times of the year. This may be true. But perhaps the meaning extends further. We now know that countless stars exist, many with Earth-like planets orbiting them. For an observer on a different planetary body—say the Moon or the Mars—the "East" and the sunrise direction will differ entirely from our own. Thus, the verse might be pointing to the multiplicity of sunrise points across the vast universe, affirming Allah SWT's sovereignty over all worlds.

Another verse highlights this:

Al-Quran 55:17 *"[He is] Lord of the two sunrises and Lord of the two sunsets."*

Traditionally, this is explained as referring to the two extreme positions of sunrise and sunset during the year: maybe. Yet modern discoveries also invite another reflection. For example, planets have been identified with binary star systems—where two suns rise and set upon the horizon instead of just one.

10. A Proper Perspective

Human beings have always wondered about their place in the vastness of existence. The Qur'an frequently reminds us that while humanity is significant, it is only a small part of a much larger reality. By inviting us to reflect on the creation of the heavens and the earth, the Qur'an expands our vision beyond the immediate concerns of our lives, urging us to consider the grandeur of Creation and the wisdom behind it. When viewed considering both faith and scientific understanding, these verses help us gain a deeper perspective on the relationship between humanity, the natural world, and the Divine.

The following verses invite us to reflect on even deeper concepts:

Al-Quran 40:57 *"Assuredly the creation of the heavens and the earth is a greater (matter) than the creation of men: Yet most men understand not."*

This is a remarkable statement, one that resonates even more with those who possess a sound understanding of the physical and natural sciences. According to one estimate, there are about 86 billion neurons in an average brain, which is a huge number, but (according to the current estimate) there are probably 100 billion trillion or more stars in the universe. When viewed through that lens, it is almost overwhelming to contemplate the vastness of time and space in which the universe unfolds. Against this unimaginable backdrop, the human being appears as a recent arrival—tiny, fragile, and only a small part of the immense puzzle of Creation.

The following verses invite us to reflect on even deeper concepts:

Al-Quran 41:9–12 *"Say: Is it that ye deny Him Who created the earth in two Days? And do ye join equals with Him? He is the Lord of (all) the Worlds. He set on the (earth) mountains standing firm, high above it, and bestowed blessing on the earth and measured therein all things to give them nourishment in due proportion, in four Days, in accordance with (the need of) those who seek (sustenance). Moreover, He comprehended in His design the sky, and it had been (as) smoke: He said to it and to the earth: 'Come ye together willingly or unwillingly.' They said: 'We do come (together), in willing obedience.' So He completed them as seven firmaments in two Days, and He assigned to each heaven its duty and command. And We adorned the lower heaven with lights, and (provided it) with guard. Such is the Decree of (Him) the Exalted in Might, Full of knowledge."*

Conceptually, these verses are profound and challenging. In my view, much of their subject matter remains beyond our current ability to fully explain. As is characteristic of the Qur'an, the sequence of details is not intended to follow a strict chronological order. For example, the reference to "Days" should be read carefully, as it metaphorically points to distinct spans of time, not simply 24-hour days.

The verses also emphasize that both *ardh* (earth/physical matter) and *samawaat* (heavens/non-physical realities) originated from a single common form—a statement strikingly consistent with modern scientific insights about the universe's origins. The role of mountains is also highlighted, inviting us to reflect on their significance. Physically, the opposite of a mountain is flat land, and mountains can be any elevation, large or small. These variations in elevation, whether dramatic or subtle, help create the conditions for water vapors to condense as rain or snow, accumulate in a stored fashion, slowly melt, seep within the soil & flow, giving rise to springs, ponds, streams, lakes, rivers, and an extensive supply of the underground reservoirs. Without this arrangement resulting from a changing landscape, water may stagnate, quickly evaporate, or remain out of reach to the land creatures, including human beings.

As for the "seven firmaments" of the *samawaat,* their exact nature remains unknown, and all interpretations so far are necessarily speculative. For instance, my earlier suggestion—that all electromagnetic waves together might represent one of these firmaments—remains just a possibility. The reality may be far greater, with dimensions still hidden from human knowledge. Allah (SWT) knows best.

Another verse offers further insight, and perhaps, considering modern scientific knowledge, brings the message closer to our understanding:

Al-Quran 41:53 *"We will show them Our signs in the universe and in their own selves until it becomes clear to them that this [Qur'an] is the truth. Is it not enough that your Lord is a Witness over all things?"*

11. The Sustenance for All Life

In this context, *ardh* and *samaa* are mentioned in the Qur'an in more than one way. On the most immediate level, the Qur'an reminds us that all physical sustenance for life emerges from this dynamic relationship: vegetation, fruits, grains, and resources growing from the earth, nourished by water descending from the sky. Rain is repeatedly emphasized as the vital link between the *samaa* and the *ardh*.

Yet the Qur'anic discourse does not stop at the surface description of rain and harvest. On deeper reflection, other verses present *samaa* in a broader and more critical sense—suggesting that the heavens are not only the source of water but also of light, heat, and regulation of time, all of which make life possible. What we now understand as sunlight driving photosynthesis, the alternation of night and day balancing ecosystems, and the winds distributing moisture and pollination—all are presented in the Qur'an as purposeful arrangements.

Al-Quran 45:5 *"And in the alternation of Night and Day, and in the fact that Allah sends down Sustenance from the sky, and revives therewith the earth after its death, and in the change of the winds—are Signs for those that are wise."*

This verse ties together multiple sustaining forces: time cycles, rainfall, renewal of dead earth, and the winds. Each of these is not random but part of a divinely ordered system.

Other verses further expand this theme:

Al-Quran 23:18-19 *"And We sent down from the sky water in due measure, and We lodged it in the earth—and indeed We are able to take it away. Then We produced for you thereby gardens of date-palms and grapes, wherein is much fruit for you, and from them you eat."*

Al-Quran 50:9-11 *"And We sent down blessed rain from the sky and made grow thereby gardens and grain of harvest, and tall palm trees with spathes piled one over another—as provision for the servants."*

Al-Quran 15:22 *"And We send the winds fertilizing, then We send down water from the sky and give it to you to drink, and you are not its storers."*

Taken together, these verses highlight a holistic view: The *ardh* provides the foundation for life, but it cannot fulfill its role without the continuous input from the *samaa*—rain, sunlight, wind, and cycles of time. Modern science helps us to glimpse the layers of meaning: the water cycle, photosynthesis, pollination, and atmospheric balance all serve as signs pointing toward divine wisdom. Sustenance in the Qur'an is not merely about food but about the integrated balance of cosmic and earthly forces.

12. Life Beyond Planet Earth

Human beings have long been fascinated by the idea of life beyond our own world. In addition to the verses discussed earlier and their expansive subject matter, the Qur'an offers suggestions that invite us to think beyond conventional boundaries—such as in the following verse:

Al-Qur'an 42:29 *"Among His signs is the creation of the heavens and the earth, and what He spread between them of all living creatures. And He is Most Capable of bringing them together whenever He wills."*

At a basic level, heavens and the earth in this *ayah* may be taken as the earth and the sky that we humans can see, and that is the way translators usually interpreted it. In terms of "living creatures", some included angels and *jinns* in this group, in a way expanding the scope of the underlying message of the *ayah*. But as I elaborated above, concepts of heavens (*samawaat*) or the earth (*ardh*) cannot be restricted to the present human understanding, or our understanding of the universe at one time of our history. What we thought about the universe or the heavens few hundred years ago was very different from now. Regardless of how one understands *samawaat*—whether as the skies, the heavens, the vast cosmos, or realms beyond the purely physical—the message of this verse is striking. It speaks of living creatures spread throughout creation, implying that life, as we know it, may not be confined to the planet Earth alone. This opens the door to a profound possibility: Life might exist on other worlds, with their own rhythms of sunrise and sunset, under the stars we have yet to see.

13. There is an End to All Creation

The Qur'an reminds us that all creation is finite and destined for an appointed end:

Al-Qur'an 46:3 *"We have not created the heavens and earth and all that is between them except for a true purpose and for a set term, yet those who disbelieve turn away from what they have been warned of."*

Al-Qur'an 39:5 *"He created the heavens and the earth for a purpose. He wraps the night around the day and wraps the day around the night. And He has subjected the sun and the moon, each orbiting* *for an appointed term. He is truly the Almighty, Most Forgiving."*

The celestial movements described here align with our scientific understanding of orbits. The Earth circles the Sun, and the Moon circles the Earth—together moving in elliptical paths shaped by the delicate balance of gravity and motion. These forces, though stable on a human timescale, are not eternal. They shift gradually, leading physicists to conclude that even the Sun, along with its planets, will one day reach an end.

Al-Qur'an 57:1–4 *"Whatever is in the heavens and the earth glorifies Allah, for He is the Almighty, All-Wise. To Him belongs the kingdom of the heavens and the earth. He gives life and causes death. And He is Most Capable of everything. He is the First and the Last, the Most High and Most Near, and He has perfect knowledge of all things. He is the One Who created the heavens and the earth in six Days, then established Himself on the Throne. He knows whatever goes into the earth and whatever comes out of it, and whatever descends from the sky and whatever ascends into it. And He is with you wherever you are. For Allah is All-Seeing of what you do. To Him belongs the kingdom of the heavens and the earth. And to Allah all matters are returned."*

In this passage, the opening line may also be rendered as "whatever is among the heavens and the earth," which broadens the scope to include all that exists within and between *ardh* and *samawaat*. Furthermore, the verse distinguishes between their individual nature. The *ardh* is described in terms of what enters and emerges from it—physical processes tied to material existence—while the *samawaat* are expressed in terms of what descends and ascends, suggesting immaterial things or realities such as divine guidance, inspiration, or physically unseen forces. Together, these descriptions encompass both the physical and non-physical dimensions of creation, as far as human understanding can reach.

14. *Ardh* and *samawaat* in the Afterlife

Reflecting on the following verses presents yet another intellectual challenge in understanding the concepts of *ardh* and *samawaat*. The following *ayat* describe a scene from the Afterlife:

Al-Qur'an 11:105–108 *"When that Day arrives, no one will dare speak except with His permission. Some of them will be miserable, others joyful. As for those bound for misery, they will be in the Fire, where they will be sighing and gasping, staying there forever, as long as the heavens and the earth will endure—except what your Lord wills. Surely your Lord does what He intends. And as for those destined for joy, they will be in Paradise, staying there forever, as long as the heavens and the earth will endure—except what your Lord wills—a generous giving, without end."*

These verses paint a vivid picture of the Afterlife, when judgment has been rendered and human destiny determined. Humanity is divided into two groups: the failed and the successful, the miserable and the joyful, or—as another translator puts it—the wretched and the blessed.

The reference to *ardh* and *samawaat* here provides a sense of time or continuity— "as long as the heavens and the earth will endure." However, the *ardh* and *samawaat* of that Day may resemble, but not identical, to those we know in our current existence. This is supported by the following verse, among others, indicating that the *ardh* and *samawaat* as we know them will cease to exist on that Day:

Al-Qur'an 14:48 *"Watch for the Day when the earth will be changed into a different earth, and the heavens as well, and all will appear before Allah—the One, the Supreme."*

The exact nature of this transformed *ardh* and *samawaat*, how they will change, and what their final state will be remains beyond our understanding. These are matters of the Afterlife—core elements of Islamic belief—mysteries that lie beyond the reach of our present human experience.

This analysis shows that the concepts of *ardh* and *samawaat* in the Qur'an represent diverse messages. I have offered several interpretations, but much remains to be explored.

Continued study may reveal further meanings as our knowledge advances. Understanding will improve with ongoing reflection, if Allah (SWT) permits.

15. Pathways in sky

Al-Quran 51:7 “By the sky with (its) numerous Paths.” The term “hubuk” has been variously interpreted as ripples or pathways, evoking images like waves in sand or water. Its exact meaning is unclear, possibly suggesting paths to different dimensions or universes. Ultimately, only Allah SWT knows the true meaning.

www.ingramcontent.com/pod-product-compliance
Lightning Source LLC
LaVergne TN
LVHW010922110826
845149LV00013B/2444